D1396591

The study of Russian history from British archival sources

The study of Russian history from British archival sources

Edited by Janet M. Hartley

Mansell Publishing Limited
London and New York

First published 1986 by Mansell Publishing Limited
(A subsidiary of The H.W. Wilson Company)
6 All Saints Street, London N1 9RL, England
950 University Avenue, Bronx, New York 10452, U.S.A.

© School of Slavonic and East European Studies, 1986

All rights reserved. No part of this publication may be reproduced or
transmitted in any form or by any means, electronic or mechanical,
including photocopy, recording or any information storage or retrieval
system, without permission in writing from the publishers or their
appointed agents.

British Library Cataloguing in Publication Data

The Study of Russian history from British archival
    sources.
    1.   Soviet Union—History—Archival resources—
    Great Britain
    I.   Hartley, Janet M.
    947   DK43

    ISBN 0–7201–1784–4

Library of Congress Cataloging in Publication Data

Main entry under title:

The Study of Russian history from British archival
    sources.

    "Papers ... read at a conference on 'The Study of
Russian History from British Archival Sources,' held at
the School of Slavonic and East European Studies,
University of London, on 11–13 April 1984"—P.
    1.   Soviet Union—History—Sources—Congresses.
2.   Soviet Union—Archival resources—Great Britain—
Congresses. I.   Hartley, Janet M.
DK3.S88   1985   947   85–21591
ISBN 0–7201–1784–4

Printed in Great Britain by
Whitstable Litho Ltd., Whitstable, Kent

Contents

Contents

Introduction

This volume consists of the papers which were read at a conference on 'The Study of Russian History from British Archival Sources' held at the School of Slavonic and East European Studies, University of London, on 11–13 April 1984. The aim of the conference was to demonstrate the richness and variety of sources in Britain for the study of Anglo-Russian and Anglo-Soviet relations and Russian and Soviet history and to show how these sources could be used as a basis for scholarly research in many fields. The theme of the conference arose from the research project to prepare a guide to documents and manuscripts in the United Kingdom relating to Russia and the Soviet Union which is being undertaken at the School of Slavonic and East European Studies and which is funded by the Leverhulme Trust.

Since the establishment of formal diplomatic relations between Britain and Russia in 1553, contacts between the two countries have been of interest to many historians. The early records relate primarily to the interests of a small sector of the British business community and to individuals who sought their fortune in the Tsar's service, but as Britain and Russia developed into great empires their relations with each other became of vital significance for all of Europe and for many parts of Asia, and this importance was reflected in an increasing amount of diplomatic, military, naval and commercial records. At the same time, scientific, intellectual and cultural contacts between the two countries expanded. Russia had provided opportunities for British traders and soldiers from the sixteenth century, and in later centuries was host to many Britons including industrialists, explorers, travellers, doctors, scientists, missionaries and members of left-wing and labour organizations. The flow was not all in one direction, and a tradition was soon established whereby Russians came to Britain to study and to learn and, in the nineteenth and twentieth centuries, to live as exiles from a regime which they could no longer accept.

The long-standing contacts between Britain and Russia in many fields have resulted in the accumulation of extensive archival material in this country. However, the location and content of this material are not always known to scholars and many collections have not been fully explored. This is partly because of the lack of appropriate finding aids, but also because the diversity of the contacts between the two countries has meant that material relating to Russia can be found in a large number of repositories, including the archives of professional, religious and cultural organizations, and in unexpected places and collections. Apart from the obvious value of British sources for the study of Anglo-Russian relations, the difficulties experienced by British scholars working in the Soviet Union make it imperative that sources in this country relating to Russian and Soviet foreign policy, military, economic and internal history should be made known.

The papers in this volume cover a wide chronological period and examine different aspects of the history of Russia and the Soviet Union, but are all based on documentary material in Britain. The papers by Professor Cross and Professor Phipps demonstrate the different reasons why Britons sought to visit and reside in Russia in the seventeenth and eighteenth centuries and the wide variety of sources in Britain relating to their activities, including travel accounts, memoirs, diaries, private papers, East India Company papers and the State Papers series in the Public Record Office. The papers show that such records are useful not only because they provide information about the British community in Russia but also for the insight they give into the Russian way of life and Russian policy towards foreigners. Dr Dukes's paper shows how the archival material of one part of Britain, north-east Scotland, can be a rich source for the study of families with strong and long-lasting connections with Russia, in particular the Gordon, Keith and Leslie families.

These papers are balanced by Mr Slatter's examination of the sources relating to the large émigré Russian community in Britain in the second half of the nineteenth century and the early twentieth century.

The papers by Dr Black, Dr Appleby and Professor Batalden demonstrate the variety of sources in Britain relating to Russia and the Soviet Union. Although the series State Papers, Russia, at the Public Record Office, is the most obvious source for diplomatic material relating to Russia before 1782, Dr Black draws attention to important additional material in the State Papers series relating to other countries, such as Sweden and Germany, and to collections of private papers in the British Library and county record offices. Dr Appleby quotes an impressive number of sources to illustrate the activities of British doctors in Russian service and the growing interest in Russian natural history in the seventeenth, eighteenth and early nineteenth centuries. The records of the British and Foreign Bible Society relating to Russia and the Soviet Union are extensive, as Professor Batalden's paper on its work in post-revolutionary Russia demonstrates.

Surveys of material relating to Russia and the Soviet Union and an active policy of collecting Russian-related material can assist and encourage the type of research discussed in these papers. Reports are included of the survey of Cyrillic manuscript codices in the British Isles by Dr Cleminson, the survey of documents and manuscripts in the United Kingdom relating to Russia and the Soviet Union by Dr Hartley, and the Leeds Russian Archive by Mr Davies. The concluding paper, by Professor Grimsted, comments on the need to be aware of the corresponding papers in the Soviet Union relating to all topics discussed in this volume.

I should like to thank the Ford Foundation for their grant towards the cost of this conference, the Director of the School of Slavonic and East European Studies for making available the facilities of the School, Dr W. F. Ryan and Dr J. E. O. Screen for editorial advice and assistance, the chairmen and all those who attended the conference and contributed to the discussions.

Janet M. Hartley

The Union Catalogue of
Cyrillic Manuscript Codices
in the British Isles
(The Pennington Catalogue)

RALPH CLEMINSON

This project grew out of an idea which was first put forward at the formation of the Slavonic and East European Mediaeval Studies Group in 1974. It was left in the hands of the late Professor Anne Pennington who, among her many other commitments, found time to look at some manuscripts, chiefly in the Bodleian Library, over the next few years. In 1978 she conducted a preliminary survey of the most promising institutions, the results of which were published the same year in the first issue of *Polata k"nigopis'naya*.

In 1980 a grant was made to the project by the British Academy from its Small Grants Research Fund, enabling Professor Pennington to give more time and attention to this line of research, and also to employ me as her research assistant. We carried out a survey of all the collections we could think of which seemed likely to have anything of the sort we were interested in, sending out over 500 enquiries to schools, universities, cathedrals, stately homes etc. The resultant replies helped us to identify *c.* 190 items distributed amongst twenty-seven collections.[1] We then proceeded to work out a method for describing the manuscripts, and thence to the actual work of description.

In 1981 Professor Pennington died. I continued to work in very uncertain conditions, and the survival of the project was really ensured by the efforts of J.S.G. Simmons, Dr M.A. Branch and Dr W.F. Ryan, to whom jointly and severally we owe the creation of a financial and administrative framework that allowed the work to continue. It was at this time that it was decided that the catalogue should be published as a memorial to Professor Pennington. The actual description of the manuscripts remained in my hands; I also inherited Professor Pennington's notes concerning some of the manuscripts in the Bodleian which, having been made at various times over many years, had no consistent form and in which, as is inevitable in the papers of a deceased scholar, it was impossible always to distinguish first impressions from final conclusions. It was therefore necessary for me to examine the Bodleian material afresh, making use of the material I had inherited for the purposes of comparison.

At the time of writing about two-thirds of the descriptions are complete, and work is progressing under the auspices of an editorial committee composed of a number of scholars with interests in the field, in which the element directly concerned with the progress of the catalogue is an executive committee comprising Dr Branch, Dr Ryan, Dr V. M. Du Feu and myself. Publication is scheduled for the summer of 1986, and is expected to take place under the aegis of the School of Slavonic and East European Studies. We are hoping to cover publication costs by means of an appeal which will make the volume a genuine memorial to Professor Pennington and to which all scholars and others who wish to honour her memory will have had the opportunity of contributing.[2]

The scope of the catalogue extends basically to all Cyrillic manuscript codices in collections in the British Isles, and these make up 159 of the 204 items included. We are also including fragments of such codices and also additions and inscriptions in Cyrillic in manuscripts in other scripts. In addition, there are thirteen rolls that are not really documents or archival materials in Dr Hartley's sense, and which we are therefore including here *da ne zabveniyu predani budut*. Eleven of these are calligraphic rolls, specimens of the writing master's art; the others are, MS Bodl. Rolls 24, a *pomyanik*, and BL Add. MS 8160, a *firman*.

The provenance of the manuscripts reflects English contacts with *Slavia Orthodoxa* over the centuries, a large majority being Russian—which almost invariably means Great Russian, and with a strong northern element, reflecting the trade route to Moscow via Archangel and Kholmogory—and a much smaller proportion from the Balkans. There are also a few home-produced ones, which include the important glossaries of Mark Ridley and Richard James.

The language of the manuscripts reflects their origins, the overwhelming majority being in Church Slavonic (of the Russian, Serbian or Bulgarian recensions), but there are a few in Russian and one or two in Rumanian.

The distribution of manuscripts by date also clearly reflects the history of these islands' relationship with their producers, the large number of Russian manuscripts of the sixteenth and seventeeth centuries reflecting the flourishing trade between England and Russia in that period. (After the end of the seventeenth century, of course, people tended to bring back printed books rather than manuscripts.) Paradoxically, the earliest manuscripts were mostly acquired later, with the more deliberate acquisition policies of large collections, notably the British Museum, in the nineteenth century, and the activities of private collectors such as Curzon, Canonici and Chester Beatty, all of which tend towards the collection of fine or old manuscripts rather than the oddments that were liable to accumulate (notably in the Bodleian) in earlier years. It also means that the preponderance of Russian over Balkan material for this period is less pronounced. The quantity of modern material is very small, and generally not very interesting, though we do have a Turgenev autograph (British Library Add. MS 40640, the juvenile poem 'Steno').

Between them the Bodleian and the British Library account for nearly two-thirds of the items in the catalogue, the latter having slightly more. The only other two collections to reach double figures are the John Rylands University of Manchester Library with ten and the Chester Beatty Library with twelve. (It should perhaps be added that there are eighteen items in Cambridge, but divided among seven collections.)

All the manuscripts are described *de visu*. Each item begins with a physical description of the manuscript, including its dimensions, the type of paper and ink used, the binding, palaeographical details etc. The contents are enumerated in detail, with incipits and explicits given for every item except where this would plainly be superfluous, as in the case of the books of the Bible. The language in which the various items are written is briefly characterized, any inscriptions in the manuscript are reproduced, and finally if anything is known of the provenance and history of it, this is also adduced. It is hoped that from such descriptions, scholars may in future be able to gain a full idea of the nature of British and Irish holdings and of their relevance to their work.

Notes

1. The eventual figure was 204 items in 31 collections.
2. Since this paper was written the project has advanced and the catalogue is soon to go to press. The appeal for funds was very successful.

The Survey of Documents and Manuscripts in the United Kingdom Relating to Russia and the Soviet Union

JANET M. HARTLEY

A survey of documents and manuscripts in the United Kingdom relating to Russia and the Soviet Union is taking place at the School of Slavonic and East European Studies. The project is funded by the Leverhulme Trust, and it is anticipated that the survey will be completed and prepared for publication by the end of 1985. The aim is to record systematically for the first time the location of all types of documentary material relating to Russia and the Soviet Union in repositories and private collections in the United Kingdom.[1] It is confidently expected that the result of this survey will be to make known the richness and variety of sources in this country for the study of many aspects of Russian history and Anglo-Russian relations, and to encourage and facilitate research in many fields. It is felt that the findings of the survey will be of great interest not only to Russian specialists, but also to general historians, linguists, social scientists and academics from many other disciplines.

Originally, the survey covered material in Great Britain but, after a substantial collection in the Public Record Office of Northern Ireland was recorded, the title of the project was changed to 'the United Kingdom'. Material relating to non-Russian nationalities and territories (the Ukraine, Caucasus, Baltic States etc.) has been included after these areas became part of the Russian Empire. Documents relating to Poland and Finland have only been included when they relate to an aspect of Russian administration in these countries. Material concerning what was Russian America, now Alaska, has also been noted. For example, a notebook of observations and calculations of magnetic declination made at Sitka, Russian America, November 1850, was recorded in the National Maritime Museum.[2] There has been no restriction about the language of the records, and material has been recorded not only in European languages, but also in Mongolian, Kalmuck, Chinese and Japanese.

As a general rule 1553, the year in which formal relations were established between England and Russia, has been taken as the starting point for the survey. A small amount of material from an earlier date has found its way into British repositories, and documents of a historical nature have been recorded. There is no terminal date for the survey, although it has not been possible to cover comprehensively material from the 1950s onwards. The thirty-year rule which operates in many repositories means that more recent papers are often not available for consultation or have not yet been listed, and many important recent papers are still in private hands.

The definition of the type of material which could be included in the survey was deliberately kept as wide as possible. All types of unpublished material have been recorded, including official reports and memoranda, government papers, commercial records and accounts, private papers, correspondence, diaries, literary manuscripts, photographs, manuscript maps and plans, manuscript musical scores, and photocopies and microfilms of manuscript material. Manuscript material of a non-historical nature, such as codices, Holy Scriptures and the lives of saints, has not been included, as these are being described in greater detail in a union catalogue of Cyrillic manuscripts and codices in British and Irish collections.[3] Typescripts and proofs of published works have been included, although pressure of space has meant that it has not always been possible to list typescript articles in detail. Major collections of newspaper cuttings have been cited, but not listed in detail. Several repositories, for example the BBC Hulton Picture Library and the Imperial War Museum, hold enormous collections of photographs of Russia. It would clearly not be practical to list all these individually, but a general description of the collections has been made. A variety of illustrative material has been included in the survey including postcards, engravings, architectural plans, shipping designs, industrial designs, lantern slides and military sketches, although paintings have been excluded.

Circular letters were initially sent to all record offices, major public libraries, university libraries and city museums. The letter included a note of material which was already known to be located in the repository. The scope of the enquiry was later broadened to include all regimental museums with records of regiments which were awarded battle honours in the Crimea and the Allied intervention in Russia, firms with strong contacts with Russia and the Soviet Union, high-street and merchant banks, insurance companies, chambers of commerce, port authorities, learned societies, scientific, medical, artistic and cultural associations, political parties, trade unions, newspapers, church, missionary and charitable organizations and a variety of societies and organizations which had connections with Russia and the Soviet Union. Notices were also placed in archive, library and museum bulletins, newsletters of associations of Russian historians and Slavists, newsletters of cultural associations connected with the Soviet Union, the *Times Literary Supplement* and *Historic House*.

Over 800 enquiries have been sent out and approximately 340 positive replies received. The response to the circular letters varied considerably. County and municipal record offices were the most efficient (although one record office failed to supply its name and address with its reply), but very helpful replies were also received from university libraries, and religious and scientific organizations. Inevitably, greater difficulty was experienced with repositories without full-time or professional staff, such as regimental museums and small social and cultural associations. By far the worst response came from firms: out of the ninety-one which were circularized, five returned positive replies, twenty-nine returned negative replies and the remaining fifty-seven failed to reply at all. It seems to be the policy of many firms to destroy old records and to regard recent material as confidential, and it was perhaps significant that those which were willing to be included in the survey were comparatively small concerns, while large organizations felt unable to co-operate.

It has proved to be very difficult to locate papers in private hands. It had been hoped that advertisements in newspapers and the newsletters of cultural groups associated with the Soviet Union would provoke some response but the results were very disappointing. Unfortunately, the survey is being conducted too late to pick up the papers of first-generation Russian émigrés and many papers have been dispersed or destroyed. The papers of British diplomats and soldiers relating to Russia have been easier to trace and some significant collections recorded, particularly relating to the Allied intervention in Russia. At the moment, eighteen private collections have been recorded, and these will form an appendix to the survey.

It was particularly satisfying to discover material relating to Russia in unexpected places. Who would have thought that Halifax Central Library (Calderdale Archives Department) and Uppermill Branch Library in Oldham would hold material relating to the wool trade with Russia,[4] that Kirkcaldy Museum would have records of voyages to Russia in the nineteenth century, or that the Alpine Club would possess photographs of the Caucasus? Other unlikely repositories containing material relating to Russia include the Sudan Archive at Durham University, the Museum of Mankind, Tolson Memorial Museum in Huddersfield, the Royal Anthropological Museum, the Alexander Grey Institute of Field Ornithology and the Royal Commonwealth Society.

Material was recorded in person in most repositories in London and in major repositories such as the British Library, the National Library of Scotland, the National Library of Wales, the Bodleian Library, Cambridge University Library, the Scottish Record Office, and the Public Record Office of Northern Ireland. All repositories were visited which were unable to provide information by post, including many small repositories such as regimental museums and archives of societies and associations. It is estimated that over 100 repositories will have been visited in the course of the project and over half the material in the survey will have been recorded through a visit rather than by post.

The material is arranged by repository, and within a repository in alphabetical order by title of collection. The aim of the survey has been to cover as many repositories, and as many collections within a repository, as possible. The need to keep the survey at a manageable length has meant that detailed entries for very large collections have not been practicable, and refer-

ences have been given to lists and indexes for further information where possible. There are some inevitable inconsistencies
in the way in which material has been recorded. An individual
item, such as a letter or a map, which is deposited singly, or
which constitutes the only item relating to Russia in a collection,
is given more prominence than a similar item which is one of
many records relating to Russia in a collection.

It was felt that a thorough listing of large collections of public
records relating to Russia in the Public Record Office, the House
of Lords Record Office and the India Office Library would be
far too large an undertaking for this project. It was also felt that
there was some justification for concentrating on the collections
in smaller repositories which were not so familiar to scholars.
Therefore, only a general description of the classes of documents which contain, or which might contain, records relating to
Russia has been made, and the appropriate finding aids listed.[5]
Private collections in the Public Record Office and the India
Office Library have been listed in greater detail.

It is estimated that the survey will include between 3–4,000
collections and individual items in all, and it would clearly be
impossible to attempt to evaluate the significance of all of these
documents. Nevertheless, it is possible to give some indication of
the areas in which it has been easiest to find material, and to
make some suggestions about the potential sources for research
which the survey has brought to light.

Inevitably, diplomatic material constitutes the largest category
of records in the survey. The large collections which have been
recorded in the British Library, House of Lords Record Office,
Bodleian Library and many university libraries and county
record offices are certainly already known to historians and it is
unlikely that the survey will reveal any unknown major collections. Because the names of diplomats can be easily checked in
the indexes of the National Register of Archives and because of
the existence of several published works relating to the papers of
government ministers, the location of papers in small repositories, such as those of Sir Charles Hanbury Williams in New-
port Central Library, are also familiar to historians of the
period. For the earlier period, most of the royal letters of the
sixteenth and early seventeenth centuries have been identified
and many have been published.[6]

The survey may contribute to the study of diplomatic history by drawing attention to letters by diplomats in collections of other individuals which may not have been studied, or which have no obvious relevance to diplomatic history. Several collections of diplomatic material in private hands have also been recorded, including the diplomatic correspondence of Sir Francis Oswald Lindley, Consul-General in Russia in 1918-19, and the correspondence of Sir Reginald Leeper with Litvinov.

Material relating to military and naval relations between Britain and Russia is also extensive. The main repositories for military records are the National Army Museum, Imperial War Museum, the Liddell Hart Centre in King's College, London, and regimental museums, although letters and diaries of British soldiers serving in campaigns involving Russia can also be found in many record offices and libraries. The Peter Liddle 1914–18 Personal Experience Archive at Sunderland Polytechnic holds a large quantity of records relating to the Allied intervention in Russia. Naval and Air Force records are less scattered, the majority being located in the National Maritime Museum and the Royal Air Force Museum respectively.

By far the largest quantity of military records relate to the Crimean War, including letters and diaries written by soldiers, medical records, reports from Russell, correspondent of *The Times,* and military sketches, maps and plans. Of particular interest are the Russian documents which were picked up by British soldiers at Sebastopol of which several have been noted, for example, a case report on a Russian sailor and a request for hospital supplies which are held in the library of the Royal College of Surgeons of England.[7] Crimean material can also turn up in unexpected places; the United Society for the Propagation of the Gospel, for example, retains records pertaining to chaplains sent to the Crimea.[8]

Other campaigns are less well covered, but documents have been recorded covering most Russian and Soviet campaigns, which a few examples will illustrate: the wills and bonds of Abraham Ashe and officers in the Tsar's service, 1619–1702,[9] a letter from Charles I to Sir Alexander Leslie regarding a licence for the levying of troops in Scotland for service in Russia, 1633,[10] lines of battle of the Russian fleet during Peter I's Swedish campaign, 1719,[11] papers of Count Horace St Paul relating to the Seven Years War,[12] returns of Russian troops in the Dutch Expedition 1799–1800,[13] papers relating to the struggle for independence of the Balkans from Turkey and Russian policy,[14] and documents relating to the Eastern Front in the Second World War prepared for the defence of Field Marshal Erich von Manstein.[15] There is also extensive material relating to Britons serving in the Russian forces. This is particularly rich for the seventeenth and eighteenth centuries and includes records relating to Patrick Gordon, James Bruce, James Keith, John Elphinstone, Samuel Greig and Charles Knowles.

The number of positive replies received from firms was so few that they can be listed in full: Angus Fire Armour, personal reminiscences, photographs and memoranda on the possibilities of Russian trade, 1916–24; Babcock International, account of the experiences of the manager of the Moscow Office during the First World War; Costain Petrocarbon Ltd, designs, contracts and correspondence relating to a chemical plant in Omsk in the early 1970s; Cable and Wireless, technical records, sales records, minutes of meetings and contracts relating to the laying of cables across Russia; Vickers plc, extensive material relating to ship-building business with Russia, mainly in the early twentieth century (to be deposited in Cambridge University Library). It is clear that these records do not reflect the extent of commercial relations between Britain and Russia. Banks proved to be a more successful line of enquiry and positive replies were received from the Bank of England, Lloyds and Midland Banks and the Rothschild Archives. The papers of merchant banks have also been recorded in the Guildhall Library and University College, London.

The lack of success in dealing with firms directly was to some extent compensated for by the discovery of extensive commercial records which have been deposited by firms in county and municipal records offices. The quantity and variety of commercial records in record offices exceeded expectations and suggested that one of the values of the survey will be to draw the attention of historians to these underused sources. Many commodities are covered by these commercial records, including agricultural machinery, beer, furs, guns, iron, locomotives, mining equipment, rails, saws, shipping, steel, textiles and timber. Some of these commercial collections are extensive. For example, the collection of John Crossley and Sons, Crossley carpets, held in the West Yorkshire Record Office, comprises 300 metres, of which 2 metres relate to trade with Russia. Port and harbour records also proved to be a useful source and included references to ships bringing goods from Russia. Although the records of the Muscovy Company were destroyed in the Great Fire of London, material has been recorded elsewhere relating to the Company's trade, and a large number of records survive relating to early trading contacts between England and Russia.

The major political parties and political and trade union organizations were contacted. The Labour Party Archive is by far the most significant for the study of Russia, containing extensive material relating to internal Russian and Soviet policy and conditions in Russia as well as party policy. Of particular interest are the section dealing with the visit of Bulganin and Khrushchev in 1956,[16] including the disputes within the party and the constituency parties concerning Khrushchev's speech, and a file containing memoranda by Kerenskii in the 1920s and reports from the provinces during the Russian Civil War.[17] The Conservative Party records[18] are less useful, and probably only contain passing references to Russia. A small amount of material was also recorded in the Cooperative Union Library, the Communist Party Archive, the Marx Memorial Library, the National Museum of Labour History, the Socialist Party of Great Britain and the Working Class Movement Library. Records of trade unions can be found in the Trades Union Congress and the Modern Records Centre at Warwick University, and some papers relating to visits of delegations to Russia are still held by individual unions, including the National Union of Railwaymen and the National Union of Mineworkers. The Trades Union Congress archive holds an extensive collection of reports and memoranda on many aspects of life in the Soviet Union, not exclusively relating to trade union affairs.

The Library of Political and Economic Science at the London School of Economics and Political Science, Hull University Library and the Modern Record Centre all have important and well-known collections of papers of left-wing intellectuals with connections with Russia, and material relating to Russia can also be found in the papers of the Fabian Society at Nuffield College, Oxford, and the Women's Suffrage Movement in Manchester Central Library.[19] Papers relating to Russian political émigrés in Britain, of which the Soskice papers in the House of Lords Record Office is probably the major collection, have been used by scholars, but the survey may include émigrés letters which have not yet been studied. Material in the survey relating to Bolshevik leaders is disappointingly slight, comprising only two letters from Lenin, signed Joseph Richter, relating to his application for a British Museum reading ticket and his issue slips, 1902–3,[20] and a receipt signed by Trotskii for a parcel which he had sent to the Moscow branch of the International Workers' Famine Relief Committee, 1923.[21]

One of the most fruitful lines of enquiry was the archives of missionary organizations. The records of the British and Foreign Bible Society[22] are particularly full, but material relating to Russia can also be found in the records of the Scottish Missionary Society,[23] the Council for World Mission, the Methodist Missionary Society,[24] the Baptist Missionary Society, the Society of Friends, the Society for the Propagation of the Gospel, the Society for Promoting Christian Knowledge, the Church Missionary Society and the Salvation Army. These records concern more than merely the work of these organizations in Russia. The British and Foreign Bible Society, for example, retains a lot of material about Bible translation and non-Russian languages in the Russian Empire, and missionary records are particularly useful in providing information about the distant parts of the Russian Empire, in particular Siberia and the Caucasus. The papers and correspondence of these organizations after 1917, when they were being threatened and disbanded in Russia, are a useful source for the study of Russia immediately after the Revolution and the Bolshevik attitude to foreign religious organizations. Contemporary Soviet policy towards religion can be studied in the records at Keston College.

Records relating to Catholics can be found in the archives of the English Province of the Society of Jesus, which holds records relating to Jesuit communities in Russia at the time of the suppression, and Westminster Diocesan Archives which hold material relating to the fate of Catholics after the Revolution. Extensive material relating to Anglican contacts with Russia and the USSR can be found at Lambeth Palace Library. Jewish records are extensive, the main sources being held in the Board of Deputies of British Jews and the Mocatta Library in University College, London. Records have also been found, mainly dating from the reigns of Catherine II and Paul, relating to the Order of St John of Malta and to masonic lodges in Russia.[25] Only one collection of Russian provenance relating to the church in Russia has been recorded, namely the accompts and inventories of the Monastery of the Cross on the Island of Kio on the Gulf of Onega, 1658–1725.[26]

Another successful line of enquiry was scientific and medical archives and professional associations whose records have been retained and preserved. The libraries of medical associations proved especially fruitful, and records relating to Russia have been recorded at the Royal Society of Medicine, the Royal College of Surgeons of England, the Royal College of Physicians in London, the London School of Hygiene and Tropical Medicine, the British Red Cross Society and the Nightingale School. There are also records relating to British doctors who served the Tsars, and in particular those of Drs James Mounsey and John Rogerson,[27] and the Dimsdale papers, which are still in the possession of the family, and which relate to the work of Dr Thomas Dimsdale including his inoculation of Catherine II and her family.[28]

In recent years, the Contemporary Scientific Archive in Oxford has been responsible for listing the papers of scientists, many of whom had contacts with Russia. One of the most interesting of these collections is the C. D. Darlington Papers, which are still in the process of being listed, and which include much interesting information relating to T. D. Lysenko and the ensuing conflict between geneticists. Papers of scientists may include material of a non-scientific nature. The Somerville collection, in the Bodleian Library, is an example of this, and includes correspondence between Catherine II and Admiral Samuel Greig and material relating to the Russian Greig family in the first half of the nineteenth century, as well as a letter on a scientific matter from Mary Somerville to Nicholas I.[29]

Other interesting collections of scientific records include the correspondence and data on astronomy which are held at the Royal Greenwich Observatory, correspondence relating to botanical matters held at the Royal Botanic Gardens in Kew and Edinburgh, records of scientific contacts and papers on Russian themes at the Royal Society, the Royal Society of Arts and the Royal Institution, and documents relating to birds, mammals, fossils, eggs, minerals and plants at the British Museum (Natural History). Learned societies which numbered Soviet scientists among their members were contacted[30] but this did not prove to be a fruitful line of enquiry. On the other hand, records of British scientists who were awarded medals and given membership of the Russian Imperial Academy of Sciences and diplomas from Russian universities in the eighteenth and nineteenth centuries have been recorded.[31]

The amount of material relating to religious and scientific relations between Britain and Russia exceeded expectations. Attempts to find records relating to cultural and educational contacts, the arts, literature and music did not meet with the same success, and the amount of material included in the survey does not reflect the importance of these contacts.

The Society for Cultural Relations with the USSR and the records of the British Council (in the PRO) have material on cultural exchanges. Russian teaching in Britain is documented in the departmental papers of several universities and in the papers of Slavists which have been deposited. One record of the experience of a Russian student in Britain is that of S. E. Desnitskii, later a professor of law in Moscow, who studied at Glasgow University in the 1770s and whose behaviour, 'guilty of a most gross violation of the Laws of Order and Decency in attacking Mr John Anderson, a Professor, in the public area of the College on the 8th of December last, in a very violent and affronting manner', is recorded in the archives of Glasgow University.[32] Little material relating to educational and cultural life in Russia or the Soviet Union has been found, although there are historical collections relating to education in Russia in the National Library of Wales[33] and in the papers of Nicholas Hans in the Institute of Education, London University.[34] The Basil Dean collection in the John Rylands University of Manchester Library contains material on the theatre in Russia.

Very little in the way of literary manuscripts has been recorded: three poems by Pushkin,[35] and one each by Turgenev and Esenin,[36] an unidentified fragment and a draft of a passage of an earlier version of *Resurrection* by Tolstoi[37] and a typescript of an article by Gor'kii.[38] The papers of Leonid Andreev and his sons Vadim and Daniil, are held in the Leeds Russian Archive in the University of Leeds. The British Library and the Royal College of Music hold manuscript musical scores of works by Borodin, Glazunov, Mussorgskii, Rachmaninov and Stravinskii, and there are documents relating to performances involving Russian choreographers and performers at the London Festival Ballet and Covent Garden. For the eighteenth century, there is also music by Catherine II's composer, M. Berezovskii,[39] and a translation made by Samuel Guthrie of the text of Catherine's opera *Oleg*.[40]

The project has not yet been completed and not all the material has yet been listed. No guide can claim to be totally comprehensive and it is certain that some repositories and collections will have been overlooked. Probably the full value of the survey will not be known until several years after its publication, when researchers will have had the opportunity to examine thoroughly the material which is listed. Nevertheless, the indications are that much new material will be brought to light and that the survey will make a valuable contribution to the study of many aspects of Russian history and Anglo-Russian relations.[41]

Notes

1.   There is no comprehensive survey of Russian material in this country but several guides indicate *inter alia* Russian holdings. *Sources in British Political History*, compiled by C. Cook, 6 vols (London, 1975–85, includes references to repositories holding Russian material (vol. 1) and papers of prominent individuals who had connections with Russia (vols 2–5). Also useful were: S. L. Mayer and W. J. Koenig, *The Two World Wars. A Guide to Manuscript Collections in the United Kingdom* (New York, 1976); C. Hazelhurst and C. Woodland, *A Guide to the Papers of British Cabinet Minsters, 1900–1951* (London, 1974); *Natural History Manuscript Resources in the British Isles*, edited by D. R. Bridson *et al.* (London, New York, 1980), and volumes in the series of Guides to Sources for British History published by the Royal Commission on Historical Manu-

scripts. A guide to the published and unpublished hold-
ings in British libraries relating to Russia and Eastern
Europe is provided by *Resources for Soviet, East European
and Slavonic Studies in British Libraries*, edited by G. Walker
(Birmingham, 1981), and material relating to the Crimea
is listed in N. Matthews and M. D. Wainwright, *A Guide to
Manuscripts and Documents in the British Isles relating to the
Middle East and North Africa* (Oxford, 1980).

2.   National Maritime Museum, papers of Vice-Adm. Sir
Richard Collinson, CLS/26.

3.   See paper in this volume by R. Cleminson.

4.   Listed in P. Hudson, *The West Riding Wool Textile Industry: a
Catalogue of Business Records from the Sixteenth to the Twentieth
Century*, Pasold Occasional Papers, 3 (Edington, 1975).

5.   The entry for the Public Record Office is largely based
on the article by N. E. Evans, 'Principal Sources in the
Public Record Office for the History of Russia and of
Anglo-Russian Relations', *Solanus*, 16 (July 1981), 1–14.
Mr Evans is a member of the advisory committee for this
project.

6.   In particular in Yu. Tolstoi, *Pervyya sorok let snoshenii
mezhdu Rossieyu i Anglieyu* (St Petersburg, 1875).

7.   The Royal College of Surgeons of England, documents in
Russian picked up by Dr Blenkins in Sebastopol.

8.   The United Society for the Propagation of the Gospel,
Crimean War Chaplains' Papers.

9.   Suffolk Record Office, Ipswich Branch, Abraham Ashe
Papers, SI/1/77/1–65.

10. Scottish Record Office (SRO), Privy Council, PC5/4, royal
letter to Sir Alexander Leslie granting him licence to raise
troops in Scotland for Russian service, March 1633.

11. National Maritime Museum, HSR/HF/7, document,
signed by Peter I, containing the line of battle and order of
sailing of the Russian fleet for the summer campaign
against the Swedes, 21 June 1719.

12. Northumberland County Record Office, St Paul Butler
(Ewart) MSS, MSS ZBU.B.2/3/36, 72.

13. History and Archives Section, Société Jersiaise.

14. The John Rylands University Library of Manchester, E. A.
Freeman Archive. Papers not yet listed.

15. Imperial War Museum, papers of Col. L. A. Liddell.
16. Labour Party Archives, International Department Papers *post* 1945, LP/ID/Box 7.
17. Labour Party Archives, International Department Russian Files, RUS/KER/1–2, RUS/RCW/1–29..
18. The archives of the Conservative Party are deposited in the Bodleian Library.
19. Archives Department, Manchester Central Library, Millicent Garrett Fawcett Papers, M50.
20. British Library, Additional Manuscript (BL, Add. MS) 54579.
21. National Library of Wales, papers of Revd T. E. Nicholas.
22. The papers of the British and Foreign Bible Society have recently been moved from the Society's London headquarters to Cambridge University Library.
23. The records of the Scottish Missionary Society are in the National Library of Scotland, MSS 8983–7.
24. The records of the Council for World Mission and the Methodist Missionary Society are in the Library of the School of Oriental and African Studies, University of London.
25. Records in the Museum and Library of the Order of St John, K2/26, K3/7, K7/23, and in the Library and Museum of the United Grand Lodge of England.
26. BL, Add. MS 46124.
27. SRO, Rogerson Papers, GD1/620; Mounsey letters are in Abercairny MSS, GD24/1846, and D. J. H. Campell W.S. Papers, GD253/144/5/4. Mounsey letters can also be found at the National Library of Wales in the E. G. B. Phillimore Papers, and at the John Rylands University Library of Manchester, Henry Baker Correspondence, Eng. MS 19, vols 3–8.
28. A copy of the list of the Dimsdale papers is available in Hertfordshire Record Office.
29. Bodleian Library, Somerville Collection; Fld MSFP$_2$–70–71, papers relating to Adm. Greig; MSDIP–9, letter from Mary Somerville to the Tsar, copy or draft, 5 September 1832, 24 March 1834.
30. Information in S. G. Korneev, *Sovetskie uchenye—pochetnye chleny inostrannykh nauchnykh uchrezhdenii* (Moscow, 1973).

31. For example, Bodleian Library, MS Savile e.11, diploma conferring membership of the Imperial Academy of Sciences at St Petersburg on Professor James Bradley, 23 September 1754; the Wellcome Institute for the History of Medicine, MS 5188, diploma conferring honorary membership of the University of Khar'kov awarded to Robert Barnes, 30 January 1867.

32. References to this incident can be found in the minutes of the Faculty of Law, Glasgow University Archives. See also A. H. Brown, 'S. E. Desnitskii, Adam Smith and the Nakaz of Catherine II', *Oxford Slavonic Papers*, New Series, 7 (1974), 42–59.

33. National Library of Wales, Reports on Education, NLW MS 12133D.

34. See published catalogue of the Hans Papers, *In Memoriam Nicholas Hans*, Education Libraries Bulletin Supplement 19 (London, 1975).

35. Greater London Record Office, Jersey Archives, Acc. 1128/187/29, verses by A. S. Pushkin; National Library of Scotland, Watson Collection, MS 581 no. 465, English translation of 'The Black Shawl'; Luton Hoo, The Wernher Collection, poem 'Freedom' by Pushkin.

36. BL, Add. MS 40640, poem 'Steno' by I. V. Turgenev; London Library, poem 'Pugachev' by S. Esenin, 1921.

37. BL, Add. MS 40688.

38. London Library, articles by M. Gorkii on the arrest and imprisonment of Schmidt, 1905, and article entitled 'London', 1907.

39. BL, Add. MS 24288, fol. 97.

40. BL, Add. MS 14390, Guthrie Papers.

41. Since the writing of this paper the collection of the material has been completed and publication by Mansell Publishing Ltd is expected in 1986.

The Leeds Russian Archive

RICHARD DAVIES

Over the years preceding the formal establishment of the Leeds Russian Archive on 25 May 1982, several collections of Russian and Russian-related material had been acquired by the University of Leeds and were housed in the Special Collections section of the Brotherton Library and in the administratively and financially independent Brotherton Collection within the Brotherton Library. These collections had found their way to Leeds more or less fortuitously, rather than as the consequence of a deliberate collecting policy by the Brotherton Library.

The Arthur Ransome Papers, for example, which include unpublished letters and official documents by Lenin, Trotskii, Radek, Litvinov and other leading Bolsheviks, as well as Ransome's own letters from Russia and copies of his telegrams to the newspapers for which he wrote, came to Leeds under the terms of Ransome's will. (His father was a professor of the then Yorkshire College at the time of Ransome's birth in 1884, and Ransome himself studied at Leeds and was considered for appointment to the newly-endowed Roberts Chair of Russian during the First World War.) The papers are now part of the Brotherton Collection, which also contains the Arthur Mattison Bequest, with its large collection of pamphlets on Russia and the Soviet Union produced mainly by British socialist groups before the Second World War. An isolated autograph letter by Lev Tolstoi among the Edmund Gosse Papers in the Brotherton Collection should also be mentioned in the context of material which had accumulated in Leeds accidentally.

In a less haphazard fashion, the Tuckton House and G. H. Perris Collections were acquired for the Special Collections section as a result of the research interest of a member of the Department of Russian Studies, Michael Holman, in the activities of Tolstoi's followers in Britain. Similarly, my own research led to the donation to the Brotherton Library of the Leonid Andreyev Collection and the associated Vadim and Daniil Andreyev Collections.

The presence in one of the country's major academic libraries of material acquired in the ways described above was not unusual and need not have prompted the decision to set up a specialized archive. That such a decision was taken in the course of 1981 can be attributed to two additional factors. The first was my discovery of the voluminous Raissa N. and George V. Lomonossoff Collections, which were deposited in the Brotherton Library by their owners and which were clearly going to generate more work, both in terms of archival processing and of research and publications, than could be absorbed on an *ad hoc* basis by either the Brotherton Library or the Department of Russian Studies. The second was the availability of a suitable archivist. In consequence, the idea of the Leeds Russian Archive was born.

At the time of the Archive's establishment in 1982 it was felt that, although no separate physical location was planned for the housing of Russian and Russian-related material, the exploitation of existing collections would be enhanced if they were treated as a coherent body of primary source material, and fresh material would more readily be attracted to Leeds if specialist services could be offered by an 'umbrella' organization of the kind envisaged.

The award of successive research-assistantships by the University of Leeds and the Leverhulme Trust, for specific projects based on the Leonid Andreyev and the twin Lomonossoff Collections respectively, made it possible to initiate the wider activities of the Archive in parallel with those projects. The success of the University's application for a 'new blood' lectureship in 1984, among other things for research on material in the Archive and the general supervision of the Archive's work, placed that work on a firm footing.

Considerable emphasis has been placed on publicity during

the Archive's first years: material has been exhibited on a dozen occasions since 1982. The first major exhibition, mounted to mark the Archive's establishment, included a selection of material from all the foundation collections. An exhibition of prints made from Leonid Andreyev's Lumière Autochromes (stereoscopic colour-plates) was first shown in the University Gallery in March 1983 and has subsequently been shown in various forms at the Universities of Glasgow, London, Budapest and Szeged (Hungary), at the National Theatre in Miskolc (also in Hungary), and at the National Museum of Photography, Film and Television in Bradford. Further displays of Archive material have been mounted at the University of Lausanne on the occasion of the Colloque Marina Tsvetaeva in 1982; at the Scott Polar Research Institute in Cambridge and the Institut d'études slaves in Paris on the occasions of the Second Conference of the British Universities Siberian Studies Seminar and the Colloque International sur la Sibérie in 1983; and at the University of Debrecen (again in Hungary) on the occasion of the 175th anniversary of the birth of Gogol' in 1984. A 'media show' on the life of Leonid Andreyev, which makes use of colour and monochrome slides and a film and sound-recording made in 1910, has proved a useful publicity vehicle and received seven airings up and down the country between summer 1982 and autumn 1984. Papers based on Archive holdings or describing the work of the Archive generally have been given at meetings and conferences in Lausanne, Oxford and London.

The Archive's activities and its interest in locating and, where appropriate, acquiring fresh material have been publicized locally, nationally and internationally in some eighty newspaper articles, newsletters of professional bodies, radio interviews and television broadcasts. While nearly all such appeals for information and material have resulted in useful contacts being established and in several cases have led to acquisitions, attempts at a blanket coverage of a given area have been chiefly valuable for the general awareness they create of the Archive's existence and aims.

By far the most productive way of encouraging donations, deposits and loans of material for copying has been direct contact with owners through correspondence and visits. Since May 1982 some 6,000 letters have been exchanged with individuals and institutions in Britain, France, Germany, Finland, Hungary, Poland, Czechoslovakia, the Soviet Union, Canada, the United States, Argentina, South Africa, Australia and Zimbabwe. Many of the leads pursued through correspondence have suggested themselves in the course of work on existing collections. Others have been passed on by the many colleagues who have taken the Archive's interests to heart. Following the establishment of contact by letter, over forty expeditions have been mounted, to locations as far apart as New York and Helsinki, but chiefly to Paris, London and other places in France and Britain. An encouraging number of benefactors and potential benefactors has also been able to pay return visits to Leeds.

The Archive's foundation collections could be divided into two broad categories: those containing Russian and Russian-related material which reflected Anglo-Russian relations, broadly defined (Ransome, Mattison, Tuckton House, G. H. Perris); and those containing Russian material which had been preserved by and to some extent reflected the life and work of Russians in exile (Leonid, Vadim and Daniil Andreyev, George and Raissa Lomonossoff). An examination of the full list of 150 acquisitions recorded between January 1982 and April 1985 shows a numerical preponderance of Anglo-Russian material, concentrated in the areas of commercial and industrial contacts between Britain and Russia from the mid-nineteenth century to the First World War, on the one hand, and British military involvement in the Allied intervention, on the other. Yet much of value has also been acquired from the Russian émigré community. Thus, alongside the extensive Cattley Family Papers and smaller groups of documents reflecting the experiences in Russia of textile-workers, merchants, governesses and soldiers from Britain, the Archive has been privileged to be entrusted with the Elizaveta Fen Collection, the twin archives of the young émigré writer Nikolai Bokov, and his journal *Kovcheg* (The Ark), and the remaining portions of the Ivan Bunin Papers, perhaps the most important Russian émigré literary collection that remained in private hands.

Prospects are good for further acquisitions in all the areas mentioned above, as the range of the Archive's contacts is constantly expanding and fresh material is being uncovered all the time. Yet it would clearly be foolish to pretend that the Leeds

Russian Archive could hope to rival existing repositories, particularly those in the Soviet Union and the United States, either in the scope or, more obviously, the volume of its holdings. Nor is the Archive in any significant sense in active competition with such long-established and large repositories, among many other reasons because of its limited financial and manpower resources. It is rather engaged in a mopping-up and rescue operation, which has occasionally, be it said, resulted in other institutions being recommended to owners of material as more appropriate homes for their collections. The value of the Leeds Russian Archive's work will have to be judged not in terms of the quantity of material accumulated, since that will inevitably be modest, but in terms of the quality of the publications which emerge from research on its collections.

Britons in Seventeenth-Century Russia:
an Archival Search

GERALDINE M. PHIPPS

The unexpected quantity and richness of the archival holdings relating to early Russian history prompted the writing of my article on the 'Manuscript Collections in British Archives Relating to Pre-Petrine Russia' that appeared in *Canadian-American Slavic Studies*.[1] It was hoped that other students or historians interested in the early Anglo-Russian relations would not have to duplicate my time-consuming efforts in locating useful materials. That article was written more than a decade ago and since then other scholars have called my attention to additional sources, or have published documents, often from private collections, that I was not aware of. Norman Evans at the Public Record Office continually turns up individual items of great interest, for example the accusation submitted by the Sanderson family against Colonel Alexander Leslie for the murder of his comrade-at-arms, Thomas Sanderson, and the will of a British soldier who died during the Russian siege of Smolensk in 1634.[2] John Appleby told me about the existence of the Ashe family manuscripts in the Suffolk Record Office. In a recent issue of the *Oxford Slavonic Papers*, Igor Vinogradoff published seven accounts of Russian missions to London that are preserved in the private holdings of the Cottrell-Dormer family.[3]

This paper is restricted to the reigns of the first three Romanov monarchs (1613–82). The materials for the reign of Peter the Great are more extensive than they are for the period 1553–1682. For example, in the State Papers, Russia, one of the most valuable collections for this subject in the Public Record Office, there are only three volumes (SP 91/1–3) for the first 130 years of Anglo-Russian relations, while for the forty-three years of Peter's reign there are six volumes (SP 91/4–9). Those volumes have not yet been fully investigated nor have the Petrine materials in the other archives been thoroughly examined. The period prior to 1613 has already been subjected to intensive exploration by such noteworthy scholars as Yurii Tolstoi, Inna Lyubimenko, T. S. Willan, Henry Huttenbach, Samuel Baron and Norman Evans. Many of the merchants' and diplomats' reports from the early period are readily available; some of them have been published in multiple editions. Much of the royal correspondence for that time has been printed.[4] While the publication of selected items, such as Patrick Gordon's diary or Samuel Collins's account, provide glimpses into seventeenth-century Muscovy, no systematic editing of the archival materials has taken place on the scale of that done for the earlier period. Inna Lyubimenko, Yurii Tolstoi and Sergei Konovalov have all published parts of the correspondence between the two courts, but no critical edition has ever been done for the royal letters for this period.[5] Such an edition would be useful for the historian, even if not commercially practical for a publisher. Anyone interested in the seventeenth century is confronted with the necessity of going directly to the archives and ferreting out the materials.

The available archival sources relating to the early Romanov period are of sufficient quality and quantity to allow numerous topics in Russian history to be explored. Some of these are obvious. The majority of records were kept by the government and are now in the Public Record Office or, if not relinquished by individuals upon retirement from office, they are now accessible in collections in various libraries, like the Bodleian or the British Library. Consequently, an extensive and detailed study of the formal diplomatic ties between England and Russia is possible. Even though the destruction of the Muscovy Company's records in the Great Fire of London 1666 makes a thorough analysis of the merchants' activities difficult, there still remain the Company's minute books for the years after 1666 and other material in the various archives, all of which can be exploited to produce a study of the trade between the two countries and the role of English merchants in Russia.

In a few unusual cases enough information is available for historians to produce monographs about individual Britons. Studies have been published on the Tsar's physician Arthur Dee, on the soldiers Alexander Leslie and Paul Menzies, on the merchants John Merrick and John Hebdon; however, none of these works is a complete and detailed biography.[6] Other men left accounts of their adventures in Russia and their impressions of the country, some of which have been published. Patrick Gordon's diary and his letters, at least those portions in print, reveal how one talented Scottish soldier viewed Russia and also reveal what he contributed to the modernization of the Russian army.[7] Samuel Collins, another doctor in the Tsar's employment, wrote a survey of Russia which is a devastating attack on the country, its government bureaucrats, its people and its customs.[8] Contemporary accounts of some diplomatic missions sent by English kings have been published, for instance, Guy Miege's description of the Carlisle embassy in 1663–4.[9] These ambassadors' reports can be supplemented by the articles Konovalov published in the *Oxford Slavonic Papers*.[10]

If the most obvious subjects for research are different aspects of Anglo-Russian relations, or the activities of individuals in Russia, there are also ways of extracting information from the archives that shed light on specifically Russian topics. In the letters exchanged between the monarchs of the two countries, in the ambassadorial reports, and in the governmental papers, there is a wealth of data which could be used to describe the internal workings and attitudes of the Russian diplomacy. Another example would be critical analysis of the New Trade Statute of 1667 (the *Novotorgovyi ustav*) issued by Tsar Alexis, partially in response to Russian merchants' complaints against the actions of foreign traders in Russia. A contemporary copy of that Statute is in the Harleian collection in the British Library.[11]

Yet the historian should not expect too much from the British holdings on early Russia. Working in the pre-Petrine period is as frustrating as trying to put together a gigantic jigsaw puzzle with thousands of pieces. This puzzle comes in a plain brown box with only the faintest sketch to indicate what the picture should look like and with the warning that an unknown number of pieces is missing. When the puzzle is finally assembled, parts of the picture are revealed in complete and vivid detail, while in other places holes of varying sizes are left. A nagging doubt will always remain about whether the picture accurately reflects the original scene, and the blank spots are mysteries about which only hypotheses can be offered. This comment is not intended to discourage historians from pursuing topics in this field, but rather it is meant to caution researchers not to expect the same abundance of information which may exist for the modern period and not to be too disappointed when some historical question cannot be answered. This caveat should be coupled with the suggestion that for this early period not all the material is in the most logical or accessible collections.

For this paper the Britons connected with Russia in the years 1613–82 have been divided into occupational groups. With the exception of some of the Muscovy Company merchants, these Britons all had firsthand experience in Russia. Some general comments about useful archival sources for different groups will be made, and a few individuals will be selected for further discussion. The majority of the Britons in Russia were comparatively obscure: if known to us by name, they have not left the kind of personal records that would enable us to write monographs about them, and most are identifiable only by name and profession; their accomplishments, their personalities, are all lost to the researcher. The examples in this paper are chosen from these relatively unknown persons. Each biographical sketch is designed to use a variety of archival materials to suggest where information, sometimes unexpectedly, may be found. These sketches will also illustrate topics in Russian history that might not be studied if one used the British archives only to concentrate on subjects relating to Anglo-Russian diplomatic and economic contacts.

It has become popular in some academic circles to argue that only historical data which can be quantified and computerized is worthwhile; any other approach is too old-fashioned. When the Britons directly connected with Russia are divided into different occupational groups, it becomes clear that statistics are not as useful as the current fashion would have us believe. The following numbers are offered with the warning that they represent only minima: not all of the Britons are named in the records. These figures, however, are helpful in demonstrating the proportion of Britons in the various categories. They represent those whose names appear in the collections in the British archives, in the small number of printed Russian records, and in the even smaller number of documents currently held in the Central State Archive of Ancient Acts (Tsentral'nyi gosu-darstvennyi arkhiv drevnykh aktov, TsGADA) of which photo-copies were exchanged with the Public Record Office. Some names found in the Russian records were spelled so strangely that they could not be correlated with any recognizable British name, and therefore they have been omitted. The categories are:

Merchants	263
Soldiers and sailors in Russian service	197
Doctors, apothecaries	16
Craftsmen	12
Male servants taken from England	6
Women (wives and servants)	36
Miscellaneous	10

The official representatives of the British government are not included in this tabulation of Britons in Russia. Counting am-bassadors, envoys or messengers would distort the figures given above as some individuals would have to be counted twice, or even three times. Several British diplomats, like Sir John Merrick or Sir John Hebdon, were members of the Muscovy Company who had lived for many years in Russia before they were appointed ambassadors. Other Britons, like Arthur Dee and Patrick Gordon, carried letters between the two courts and may have conducted minor diplomatic negotiations, but Dee's and Gordon's primary roles were as doctor and soldier respec-tively in the hire of the Russian Tsar. At those times when no formal representative was in Russia, the Muscovy Company's chief agent often acted for the King. And, if one wanted to count diplomats, where would one place Richard Bradshaw, a fully accredited envoy sent by Oliver Cromwell, who was never allowed to enter Russia?

The miscellaneous group includes an Ambrose Frere, a 'master of arts and preacher of God's Word, [allowed] to goe to reside in the dominions of the Emperor of Russia to preach to the English nation there',[12] and others who cannot be identified by their profession. Three of these were permitted to travel to Russia about 'their Affairs', but the nature of these affairs was not specified. And why did Richard Fowell, gentleman, George Higham, gentleman, Thomas Cowley, gentleman, and Thomas Rodes, of King's College, Cambridge, want to go to Russia?[13] The last was authorized to go there for three years 'provided he repayre not to the cittie of Rome'. Perhaps Russia was part of a Grand Tour for these young gentlemen, although this hardly seems likely. All of the men in this miscellaneous category received passes from the English government which can be found in the minute books of the Privy Council or in the series of Licences to Pass Beyond the Seas.

With the exception of the merchants, each of these categories contains persons who were in Russia, or who at least had been given permission to travel there. For the merchants the figure stands for all those men who were affiliated with the Muscovy Company, either as employees or members. While some agents, like John Merrick, were later admitted to full standing as members, others remained employees without ever achieving that status. The agents who conducted the Company's business in Russia were only a small percentage of the men connected with it. Most were merchants who never set foot in the Tsar's lands but, as was typical of the seventeenth-century commercial class in London, invested in the activities of different trading companies without ever participating in the buying or selling of goods in a foreign country. This figure of 263 merchants therefore includes men who never visited Russia but, at the same time, absent from this total are most of the employees who actually traded in Russia, who worked in the Company's rope-yards, or who performed other labour for it; their names are simply not available in the extant documents.

The destruction of the Muscovy Company records for the period before 1666 makes it difficult, but not impossible, to identify its members and to study its activities. The minute books after 1666 exist and are in the Guildhall Library. The information in these can be supplemented by materials found in the Public Record Office: in the State Papers, Foreign and Domestic, in the Port Books (E 190), the Customs Accounts (E 122), the minute books of the Privy Council, in the Colonial Office Records, East Indies (CO 77), and the various collections which preserve the royal letters and translations or drafts of letters (PRO 22/60, SP 102/49, and the Entry Books, SP 104). A researcher should know that the English royal letters are photocopies of ones held by TsGADA. When the exchange of photocopies of the royal correspondence took place, the Russians provided letters only up to 1665. For the letters sent by Stuart monarchs after 1665 one must use the drafts in the Foreign Entry Books. Other depositories also have manuscripts that are useful for the study of the Muscovy Company. Of particular value are the Cotton, Lansdowne and Additional manuscripts in the British Library, and the Ashmole, Tanner and Clarendon manuscripts in the Bodleian Library at Oxford. A search through these various archival holdings will uncover such documents as a translation of the Company's Charter of 1628 (the last given to it in the seventeenth century), reports from agents in Russia, petitions from the Company to the English government, papers about the Company's debts and financial woes, as well as a few records about its actual trade.

Personal papers of individual members of the Company are also a rich mine of information. For example, the Ashe MSS in the Suffolk Record Office not only supply data about the family's financial involvements, but they also illustrate arrangements made by Britons who entered the Tsar's service. Arthur Dee, Tsar Michael's physician, instructed Abraham Ashe to transmit money on a regular basis to London for his family's use. In the 1630s several British soldiers entrusted Ashe with their wills in case they died during the forthcoming campaigns against Poland, and others borrowed money to tide them over until they received their pay. If the Ashe MSS tell us so much about Britons in Russia, perhaps similar materials will be found in other family archives. Another useful source of personal and financial information is the wills of merchants, like Merrick and various members of the Hebdon family. Wills reveal the size and contents of the estates left by individuals, and are particularly useful for establishing genealogical as well as personal relations between Britons in Russia, and even on occasion help establish the geographical location of individuals in Russia.

The participation of the Muscovy Company merchants in the activities of other trading organizations provides another way of finding information about Britons in Russia: by checking the archives of other merchant companies in London. The Mercers' Company, for example, has lists of those of its members who were also free members of the Muscovy Company; some of these names are not found in any other records about the Muscovy Company. One archive which must be searched for mention of the Russian trade is the East India Company records at the India Office Library and Records. Many merchants invested in both companies. In 1618 the two companies entered into a joint venture to loan money to Tsar Michael, and both companies were interested in the possibility of establishing trade routes across Russia to Persia, if the Russian government could be persuaded to give them permission.

It is from the East India Company Records that the first individual to be discussed has been chosen. In these records appear several fascinating and puzzling references to an envoy sent from Russia in 1669. One mentions 'Mr Thomas Bryan, then going as Envoy from his Majesty [the Tsar of Russia] to the King of Persia, to settle the traffique of Raw Silke betweene them'.[14] In another letter this envoy was described as 'one Mr. Bryan, an English merchant that had long lived in Russia, whom the Empiror sent as his envoy extreordenary to the King of Persia, to treate about raw silk, which envoy unhappely dyed, and the greatest part of his retinue, before they arrived Spawhawne [Isphahan]'.[15] These quotations raise several questions. Who was Thomas Bryan? Why was an Englishman going to Persia as the Tsar's envoy? Does the sending of Bryan to Persia reveal anything about Russian diplomatic practices in the seventeenth century?

The earliest reference to Thomas Bryan is in a letter written in 1655 by William Prideaux, the ambassador sent by Oliver Cromwell to persuade the Russian government to restore the Muscovy Company's Charter of Privileges which had been abrogated in 1649. Prideaux asked 'If it stand with his highness's likeing, that at Archangel I open the emperor's letter, to have it there turned into English by Thomas Bryan the English merchant, that's here, and will be there at the mart, who is my confident, well versed in the Russe idiome, I believe he will do it better than any in London'.[16] This single comment suggests two things about Bryan. He had been in Russia long enough to become fluent in the language, and Prideaux considered him to be trustworthy, if not a supporter of the Cromwellian regime. In contrast, Prideaux did not trust other Britons in Russia whom he labelled the English Russes. He blamed them, particularly the Muscovy Company merchant, John Hebdon, for the failure of his mission.[17]

John Hebdon's role in Russia at that time was ambiguous. He had worked for the Muscovy Company there since at least 1640 and had occasionally performed duties for the Tsar Alexis, who had even sent him on a mission to Western Europe in 1652.[18] Some of Hebdon's actions in Russia during the interregnum and later at the time of the Stuart Restoration indicate his royalist sympathies; however, Prideaux's descriptions of Bryan and Hebdon should not be interpreted to imply any political conflict between the two men, although some may have existed. There are indications that they co-operated in conducting the merchants' affairs, on one occasion going surety for a third's business venture. It is perhaps more significant that Bryan married Hebdon's daughter, Elizabeth. After Bryan's death in Persia the Hebdon family provided for the education of his son and left legacies to Elizabeth Bryan and their children.[19]

After Hebdon returned to England in 1661, Bryan apparently became the chief agent in Russia. Because of the scarcity of the Muscovy Company records, only a few notes of his purchases of naval supplies are extant.[20] A contemporary Russian document called Bryan a tar leaseholder, which probably refers to his efforts to secure a tar monopoly for the English merchants.[21]

A more interesting aspect of Bryan's activities extended beyond his commercial transactions into the area of performing as a kind of sub-consul or minor royal official. A 1661 memorandum from the English Naval Office concerning a commission to him to transport hemp from Archangel to England referred to him as 'Thomas Bryan merchant residing as his Majesties Agent in Russia'.[22] This title seems to have exaggerated Bryan's importance, as Charles II did not call him a royal agent four years later, when the King explained in a letter to Tsar Alexis that he had charged 'our Trusty Thomas Bryan, one of Our Subjects residing in Your Imperiall Citty of Mosco' to deliver the letter.[23] It was not unusual for the chief agent to convey letters between the two governments, but it was perhaps more exceptional for Bryan also to translate the King's letters into Russian.

Four of the available letters from Charles II carry the notation that Bryan had provided the translations.[24] Bryan acted as an interpreter for Prideaux and then later for the Earl of Carlisle during his unsuccessful mission of 1663–4.[25] On that occasion Bryan had helped to organize the proper reception for the British ambassador.[26] Again none of these actions was extra-ordinary, for the Company's chief agents customarily aided British diplomats in Russia whenever necessary.

Nowhere in this collection of facts, all culled from the British archives, is there any explanation of why Tsar Alexis chose Bryan as his envoy to Persia. None of this information suggests that Bryan's political or diplomatic efforts ever exceeded those of previous agents. In fact both Sir John Merrick and Sir John Hebdon had each earlier performed more commissions for the Tsars in these areas than Bryan appears to have done. A hint of the reason behind his selection as envoy may be found in several published Russian sources. According to them, in 1667 the Tsar's official, Afanasii Ordin-Nashchokin, signed an agreement with an Armenian trading company permitting the Armenians to sell raw silk and Persian products in Russia, first to Russian merchants and then, if goods still remained, to foreigners. The company designated an Englishman, described as a long-time resident of Russia, Thomas Brein (as Bryan's name is often spelled in the Russian documents) to supervise its commerce in Moscow.[27] It can be posited that Bryan's connection with the Armenians' silk trade explains why Alexis sent him to Persia as the Russian envoy; however, nothing indicates why Bryan accepted the responsibility. Had he abandoned his Muscovy Company post and entered the Tsar's employment? Or was he still its chief agent and exploiting this opportunity to help the Muscovy Company gain an advantage in the competition with other foreigners for Persian silk?

Even if Bryan's motives remain mysterious, his appointment introduces a question which needs further exploration and for which the British archives provide much valuable data, that is, the Tsars' use of foreigners to represent Russia in negotiations with other governments. Tsars had frequently appointed foreigners to act as their agents abroad, but Bryan's situation apparently differed from these other cases. Even when a Tsar entrusted minor diplomatic commissions to British merchants, they were normally to act between Russia and England, and only rarely between Russia and some other Western European country. The Tsar usually selected foreigners to perform his diplomatic tasks from among the men who had entered his service. Three examples can be drawn from the Britons in Russia. In 1626 Arthur Dee, Tsar Michael's physician, was instructed to go to England on the Tsar's business, and he was accompanied by a Russian interpreter.[28] On the occasion of his first trip to England after entering the Tsar's army, Patrick Gordon carried letters between the two courts and met with English officials in London.[29] Another Scottish soldier, Paul Menzies, played an even larger role in Russian diplomacy. In 1662 he accompanied a Russian embassy to Persia; in 1667 he was sent to Sweden to hire miners. His most important assignment was in 1672 when Tsar Alexis was attempting to persuade other Christian monarchs to unite against the Turkish Sultan. Menzies was ordered to go to the rulers of several German states and to the Pope in Rome, while a Dutchman, Andrei Vinius, went to England on a similar mission.[30] The information in the British archives would need to be supplemented by materials in other European archives, and obviously by TsGADA records, but it should also be noted that a large number of the relevant Russian documents were published in the nineteenth century. Therefore the suggestion that Russian diplomatic practice may be studied by using the British archives is not as far-fetched as it may seem at first glance.

If the number given for the Muscovy Company, by including merchants who never visited Russia, creates the impression of more Britons there than is actually accurate, the figure for the soldiers is misleading in the opposite way, by underestimating the number. The Russian government, although it occasionally accepted a single officer into its army, preferred to hire only those accompanied by a regiment of ordinary soldiers and frequently turned down those who arrived without any troops. With the exception of the ones listed in the few account books, that is, pay registers, printed in the *Russkaya istoricheskaya biblioteka* (vol. 28) or in other Russian publications, it is impossible to identify the regular soldier or even to offer a reasonable guess at the size of the British contingent in the Russian army. One author asserted that as many as 3,000 Scottish soldiers served in

Russia, but since he cited no sources for his statement it cannot be verified.[31] In 1632 the Scottish Colonel Alexander Leslie requested permission from the English government to levy 2,000 soldiers for the Tsar, but how many men responded to his call cannot be determined from the British records.

If an examination of the Russian archives is required before any exact assessment of the number of Britons in the Tsar's armies is possible, some useful generalizations and some interesting questions can still be drawn from the British archives. Many of the document collections cited above for the Muscovy Company would also be valuable for studying the British military men. The collections of State Papers, both Domestic and Foreign, and the Privy Council minute books, the Ashe MSS, the Rawlinson MSS, and the various classes containing the royal letters must be checked. The royal letters are a major source of information about the officers. Besides indicating the qualifications of some individuals, the letters illustrate the role played by the English government in helping Britons into or out of the Russian army. Several other collections which have useful documents about an individual soldier or a specific event are noted below.

The Britons in Russian military service are clustered in three periods, each reflecting a crisis in either Russia or England. In the seventeenth century the first wave of Britons to fight in Russia arrived during the Time of Troubles when English, Scottish and Irish soldiers fought on all three sides, with the Russian, the Polish and the Swedish forces. There are very few documents referring to these soldiers, but letters in the Public Record Office State Papers, Poland (SP 88) mention several of them. Some soldiers remained in Russia after Michael became Tsar in 1613, and the wages paid them are described in the Russian account books noted above. The release of individual soldiers, like Arthur Aston, from Russia, became the subject of letters exchanged between James I and Michael, and this correspondence is preserved in the Public Record Office. Other documents about Aston, including a translation of the Tsar's letter given him upon his departure, are in the Harleian MSS in the British Library.[32]

The second and probably the largest influx of Britons into the Russian army resulted from a recruitment drive in Western

Europe in the early 1630s, when Russia was preparing for war with Poland. Alexander Leslie, who conducted that levy of soldiers, received permission from the English government to raise 2,000 soldiers.[33] Even if it is impossible to determine how many Britons actually accompanied Leslie back to Russia, the role of the English government in the hiring of these men can be traced through the British archives. In a letter to Charles I, Michael accused Poland of attacks and various misdeeds against his country and asked the King to aid him by allowing Leslie to recruit soldiers. Charles responded with the promise to give 'free leave, Consent, and Libertie' to any 'Subiects in our dominions, who are willing to serve your Majestie in the quallitie of Commaunders or Souldiers'. The King demonstrated his support by writing recommendations for individual officers who wanted to join Michael's army.[34] The English Privy Council issued warrants to Leslie and other officers for raising of volunteers.[35] The Privy Council also wrote to the Corporation of Gloucester requesting that it help to find soldiers in that area; its letter and translation of the general Russian instructions for Leslie are in the Corporation's Letterbook.[36] Charles I also instructed the Scottish Privy Council to aid one of Leslie's subordinates in recruiting soldiers there.[37]

Some soldiers can be identified from other documents, for example, the Ashe MSS. Individual officers are named in the Licences to Pass Beyond the Seas for that period. It is extremely interesting to note that none of these licences was for the soldiers going to Russia; they were instead given to the wives and children who were joining the officers in Russia.[38]

If these first two large groups of Britons entering the Russian army came at times when Russia was fighting Sweden or Poland, the third wave was caused by the English Civil War. After the triumph of Oliver Cromwell and the Parliamentary forces, many royalists fled to the continent and joined foreign armies. Some, like Thomas Dalyell and William Drummond, eventually found their way to Russia. Others, like Patrick Gordon, went to Russia in the early 1660s when the disbanding of royalist armies precluded any hope of finding military employment at home. The Additional MSS in the British Museum have letters and papers about Dalyell, Drummond and Gordon. In the *Historical Manuscripts Commission's 9th Calendar* there are a few documents about

Dalyell, including a translation of the Tsar's pass dismissing him from Russian service.[39]

Although it is possible to analyse the entry into and the departure from Russian service of these Britons, their contributions to the success or failure of the Tsar's armies cannot be evaluated at this point. Other questions about the British soldiers can be suggested. The experiences of one soldier, John Scroope, illustrate two problems that confronted not only him but also other Britons living in Russia. What were the barriers to leaving the Russian army? And what was the significance of the adoption of the Orthodox religion by a non-Russian?

John Scroope entered Russian service in 1615, spent some time in Kazan, and was eventually transferred to duty in Moscow. In 1622, in response to pleas from 'the friends and kindred' of Scroope, James I wrote to Michael, requesting that he dismiss the soldier and allow him to return to England.[40] Michael refused and claimed that Scroope himself had petitioned to remain in Russia and that the Englishman received an estate and a large salary because he had enrolled in the Tsar's army *'na nashe gosudarskoe imya'* and of his own free will.[41] The Tsar's answer apparently ended the efforts to secure Scroope's dismissal. Five years later a George Verney approached the English Secretary, Sir John Coke, on behalf of 'one John Scroope sonne of Sir Adrian Scroope, knight, who now serveth the Emperor of Russia and is in his pay in the hopes of advancement', for Scroope's only desire was to have 'letters of testimonial under his Majesties hand to certifie that hee is of a noble familie and sonne of a Knight and to recomend him to the favor of that state as his worth and service shal merit'.[42] Coke attempted to obtain such a letter from Charles I. There is no record of any letter being written in 1627, but two years later Charles I did recommend Scroope to Michael as being deserving of his largesse. This letter followed the format put forth by Coke, commenting on Scroope's family background and education and appealing for the continuation of the Tsar's 'good Favour and Princely Goodness towards him according to his qualitie and the merit of his services. . . .'[43] While Charles' letters may demonstrate the role of the English government in aiding individuals who wanted to enter or to leave the Russian army, it did not touch upon the Tsar's justification for refusing to accommodate his fellow monarch's request. Michael had earlier permitted other Britons to leave when the King had intervened on their behalf; why did he not agree in Scroope's case?

Two Russian historians have offered contradictory interpretations for the failure of Charles to obtain Scroope's release, and this conflict of opinion reflects the two problems mentioned earlier. A. S. Mulyukin argued that soldiers hired '*na gosudarskoe imya*' and of their own will were regarded as permanent residents, as Russian subjects.[44] His explanation fits the expressions used in Michael's letter. Scroope's fate paralleled that of other Britons who encountered difficulties when they tried to leave Russia. The decision often hinged on whether they agreed to limited, short-term service or whether they had been accepted for permanent employment. The British archives contain numerous petitions and letters about Britons' efforts to resign from the Russian army, and an examination of Scroope's and others' difficulties would provide some interesting insights into the position of foreigners there.

The second interpretation of why Scroope was unable to return to England is given by D. Tsvetaev in his monumental study on Protestants in Russia. He stated that the real reason behind the Tsar's refusal to dismiss Scroope was his marriage to a Russian woman and his acceptance of Russian Orthodoxy.[45] By these acts Scroope had acquired Russian nationality and therefore must remain in that country. Mulyukin disagreed with this opinion and asserted that the marriage would not confer Russian nationality and Scroope would still have been considered as a British subject. He also questioned if Scroope had actually accepted Orthodoxy.

The issue of whether the adoption of the Orthodox religion would prevent the convert from ever leaving Russia is raised three times in the material about Britons in Russia.[46] If Scroope resigned himself to his fate and continued to serve the Tsar, two other Britons were not as willing to accept the fact that the Tsar's government treated them as Orthodox and therefore, as Russian subjects, forbidden to go abroad. Twice the Stuart Kings demanded the return to England of English women who, the Russians claimed, had adopted Orthodoxy and, therefore, could not leave the country.

The first case was that of Ann Barnseley, the daughter of

an Englishman living in Russia. At the age of fifteen she had married a Frenchman, Pierre de Redmond, Baron de Tart. In 1628 her husband converted to Orthodoxy and tried to persuade her to do likewise, but she refused and her father supported her decision. The matter was brought to the attention of Patriarch Filaret who, in view of her youth, ordered that she was to be treated as a child and rebaptized by force if necessary.[47]

Even after this compulsory rebaptism the young Baroness did not regard herself as Russian Orthodox. In the early 1630s her husband died, and she begged for permission to return to the Protestant faith. The Russians responded by taking her sons away from her and entrusting them to a Russian nobleman to raise. She and her infant daughter were confined to a monastery. Her family and friends, both in Russia and in England, labelled her confinement as imprisonment. In December 1636 Charles I wrote to Michael requesting that she be released and permitted to return to England. For some inexplicable reason this letter was not delivered for over a year; in January 1638 the Muscovy Company agent, Simon Digby, presented it to the Tsar.[48]

The Tsar's answer, written in March 1638, implied that the King had been misinformed. Michael insisted that as the Baroness and her children had voluntarily accepted Orthodoxy, the only true religion, they could not return to their old religion nor leave the country. He denied that Ann Barnseley had been converted against her will and explained that foreigners in Russia were never forced to relinquish their own faith. Moreover, the Tsar asserted that she was not in prison, but only receiving careful instruction in the Orthodox religion.[49]

This letter was entrusted to Digby who sent it to London with a covering letter of his own. He disputed the Russian version of the incident and claimed that, although no one dared disagree with the Tsar (especially as his father, the Patriarch Filaret, had been responsible for the woman's predicament), numerous witnesses, including one of Digby's own servants, had seen her 'dragged alonge from the maide Monastrye to the river to bee Christened ... '.[50] After the arrival of the Russian letter in England, Barnseley's friends and relatives petitioned the King to renew his efforts to secure her freedom.[51]

None of the pleas of the King, the Muscovy Company, or her friends and family obtained her return to England, but the

Baroness was allowed to leave the monastery and to live in Moscow. According to a letter from Digby of 1 April 1639 (this letter is in a very obscure collection in the PRO, which contains manuscripts relating to the Digby family, and in this unlikely place is the answer about Ann Barnseley's fate):

> Mr. Barneslyes daughter is now come up to this towne and is turned Russ. She lives in her owne house, but the Emperor doth not allow her anything for the maintenance of herself and her children, so that she is forced to be kept by her Father and her friends, which is a very lamentable case.[52]

She was permitted almost complete freedom in Moscow, the only prohibition being that she not attend any non-Orthodox church services. She was never allowed to leave Russia but died there, probably in the 1640s.[53] Tsvetaev claimed here, as he had in the case of Scroope, that the issue was her conversion to Orthodoxy. In Russian eyes the question of her baptism, willingly or unwillingly, was of secondary importance to her marriage to a member of the Orthodox religion. The spouse always became Orthodox in this situation, if the marriage were to be valid in the opinion of the Russians.[54] Since the validity of her marriage was never questioned by the English, there was no possibility that the Tsar's government would ever release her.

The second case was that of Frances Rose; however, in this instance the Russians apparently allowed her to leave. Shortly after Charles II's accession, the girl's mother submitted a petition to him concerning her daughter's retention in Russia. Her husband, John Rose, had been a loyal supporter of Charles I and had lost his life during the Civil War. Unable to care for her four small children, she permitted her sixteen-year-old daughter Frances to accompany Colonel John Gibson and his wife to the continent, and they had taken her to Russia. They joined the Russian Orthodox Church and compelled the young girl to abandon her Protestant religion. Now, her mother said, Frances Rose wished to return home but was 'restrained by reason of her Religion to returne to her native Country ...'. Therefore she begged the King to intervene on her behalf.[55]

In May 1661 Charles II wrote to Alexis requesting that Frances Rose be allowed to leave Russia, and in an effort to obtain the Tsar's agreement, he promised that she would be permitted to continue to worship in the new 'religion which she now professeth'.[56] Her freedom was not to be obtained that easily. During their missions in 1663 and in 1667, both the Earl of Carlisle and Sir John Hebdon appealed to the Russian government for her release. The Russians explained to Carlisle that Frances Rose could not be given liberty to go to England.[57]

Neither Carlisle nor Hebdon obtained her freedom, yet it is interesting to note that she was allowed to leave a few years later. Sometime in the 1670s a Polish soldier, Jacob Melosky, petitioned both the King and the Secretary of State, Lord Arlington, for aid in finding employment, and he went on to explain that he had rescued his wife, Frances Rose, from Russia where she 'had lived in Slavery and Bondage for the space of seventeene yeares ... '. Melosky, who had served the Tsar, relinquished his military command there in order to 'sett her at Liberty for the enjoyment of the Protestant Religion', and he had brought her to England.[58] There is no information, except his petitions, to indicate that the Russians had reversed their usual position about not letting Orthodox Christians leave the country. Nor is it possible to determine why an exception was made in her case.

The three cases of Scroope, Barnseley and Rose demonstrate that, by using the British archives, problems confronting foreigners who adopted Orthodoxy can be explored. Other information dealing with the practice of their religion by foreigners might also be put forward. From the pass given to Ambrose Frere, it is clear that on at least one occasion a Protestant minister went to Russia to care for the Britons there. The Muscovy Company maintained its own chapel within its facilities in Moscow. A careful reading of Patrick Gordon's diary might provide enlightenment about how a devout Catholic fared in the observation of his faith in Russia.

It was stated earlier in this paper that the discussions about individuals would centre on relatively unknown persons, and there is no more obscure group than the British women, wives and daughters who followed their husbands and fathers to Russia. The passes allowing these women to go to Russia and the petitions by and about them indicate that it was quite common for the Muscovy Company merchants, the medical experts, the craftsmen and the soldiers to take their families with them and to establish their homes there. The role of these women has never been studied. If a detailed study of the development of the Foreign Quarter is ever written, perhaps more will be known about this side of the life of Britons in Russia.

In the meantime a study of the references to British women in Russia opens up aspects of Russian social or legal history that would not ordinarily be raised in the context of Anglo-Russian relations. For example, on at least two occasions English women submitted petitions to the Russian government demanding redress for crimes or grievances committed against their husbands by other foreigners. In 1633 Judith Sanderson presented an accusation to the 'High Courte of Warre' in Moscow against Alexander Leslie for his murder of her husband, Thomas Sanderson; the response of the Russian government is unknown.[59] Forty years later Mary Hebdon, supported by her son-in-law, Samuel Meverell, submitted petitions to the Russian government in answer to the statement of another foreign woman that she was owed money from the estate of Mary's husband, Thomas Hebdon, even though the Russians had rejected her direct claim against Thomas ten years earlier. The Hebdon case dragged through the Russian bureaucracy for years, and the English government finally intervened.[60] Although such isolated incidents as are represented by the Sanderson and the Hebdon cases may not actually be too important in themselves, they raise an interesting question. At a time when Russian women had no public role and few rights, would a study of how the Russians treated foreign women, since it obviously was forced to deal with them or their representatives, lead to a new understanding of seventeenth-century Russia?

I would like to conclude with this wild speculation and with just one additional comment. There are more ways of using the British archives about pre-Petrine Russia than many of us historians have considered. If we stop focusing on Anglo-Russian relations, we may find it possible to draw some valuable generalizations about Russia.

Notes

1. Geraldine M. Phipps, 'Manuscript Collections in British Archives Relating to Pre-Petrine Russia', *Canadian-American Slavic Studies*, 6, no. 3 (Fall 1972), 400–15.

2. Public Record Office (PRO), SP 80/9 fols 8r–9v, A Declaration … against Collonell Allexander Lesseley … ; Prob 11/167 fols 30r–31v, Will of Richard Coningsby, 23 January 1634.

3. Igor Vinogradoff, 'Russian Missions to London, 1569–1687', *Oxford Slavonic Papers* (*OSP*), New Series, 14 (1981), 36–72.

4. Inna I. Lyubimenko, *Istoriya torgovykh snoshenii Rossii s Angliei* (Yur'ev, 1912); E. Delmar Morgan and C. H. Coote (eds.), *Early Voyages and Travels to Russia and Persia*, 2 vols (London, 1886); *Pamyatniki diplomaticheskikh snoshenii Moskovskago gosudarstva s Anglieyu*, vol. 38 of *Sbornik imperatorskago Russkago istoricheskago obshchestva* (1883); Yurii Tolstoi, *Pervyya sorok let snoshenii mezhdu Rossieyu i Anglieyu* (St Petersburg, 1875); Lloyd E. Berry and Robert O. Crummey, *Rude and Barbarous Kingdom* (Madison, 1968).

5. S. Konovalov, 'Seven Letters of Tsar Mikhail to King Charles I, 1634–8', *OSP*, 9 (1960) 32–63; S. Konovalov, 'Seven Russian Royal Letters (1613–1623), *OSP*, 7 (1957), 118–34; S. Konovalov 'Twenty Russian Royal Letters', *OSP*, 8 (1958), 117–56; I. Lyubimenko, 'Letters Illustrating the Relations of England and Russia in the Seventeenth Century', *English Historical Review*, 32 (1917), 92–103; Yurii Tolstoi, 'Spiski s Tsarskikh gramot khranyashchikhsya v Londonskom Korolevskom arkhive', *Chteniya v imperatorskom Obshchestve istorii i drevnostei rossiiskikh*, II (1864), 12–32.

6. John H. Appleby, 'Dr Arthur Dee: Merchant and Litigant', *Slavonic and East European Review*, 57, no. 1 (1979), 32–55; J. H. Appleby, 'Some of Arthur Dee's Associations Before Visiting Russia Clarified, Including Two Letters from Sir Theodore Mayerne', *Ambix*, 26, no. 1 (1979), 1–15; N. A. Figurovski, 'The Alchemist and Physician Arthur Dee (Artemii Ivanovich Dii): An Episode in the History of Chemistry and Medicine in Russia', *Ambix*, 13, no. 1 (1965), 35–51; 'Poslanie shvedskogo polkovnika Aleksandra Lesli k tsaryu Mikhailu Feodorovichu', edited by E. F. Budde, *Pamyatniki drevnei pis'mennosti i iskusstva*, 165 (1906); Paul Dukes, 'The Leslie Family in the Swedish Period of the Thirty Years' War', *European Studies Review*, 12 (1982)

401–24; N. V. Charykov, *Posol'stvo v Rim i Sluzhba v Moskve Pavla Meneziya* (St Petersburg, 1906); Geraldine M. Phipps, *Sir John Merrick, English Merchant-Diplomat in Seventeenth-Century Russia* (Newtonville, Mass., 1983); I. Ya. Gurlyand, *Ivan Gebdon, Kommissarius i rezident* (Yaroslavl', 1903).

7. Patrick Gordon, *Passages from the Diary of General Patrick Gordon of Auchleuchries* (Aberdeen, 1859); S. Konovalov, 'Patrick Gordon's dispatches from Russia, 1667', *OSP*, 11 (1964), 8–16; S. Konovalov, 'Sixteen Further Letters of General Patrick Gordon', *OSP*, 13 (1967),72–95.

8. Samuel Collins, *The Present State of Russia, In a Letter to a Friend at London* (London, 1671).

9. Guy Miege, *A Relation of Three Embassies from his Sacred Majestie Charles II to the Great Duke of Muscovia, the King of Sweden, and the King of Denmark, Performed by the Right Honorable the Earl of Carlisle in the Years 1663 and 1664* (London, 1669).

10. S. Konovalov, 'Anglo-Russian Relations, 1617–1618', *OSP*, 1 (1950), 64–103; S. Konovalov 'Anglo-Russian Relations 1620–24', *OSP*, 4 (1953), 71–131; S. Konovalov, 'England and Russia: Three Embassies, 1662–5', *OSP*, 10 (1962), 60–104; S. Konovalov, 'England and Russia: Two Missions, 1666–1668', *OSP*, 13 (1967), 47–71.

11. British Library (BL), Harleian MSS 6356.

12. *Acts of the Privy Council of England, 1627 January to August* (*APC*) (London, 1938), p. 346.

13. *APC, March 1625 to May 1626* (London, 1934), p. 108; *APC, July 1628–April 1629* (London, 1958), p. 414; PRO, PC 2/44 fol. 620, pass for George Higham, 17 June 1635; PC 2/45 fol. 99, pass for Thomas Cowley, 27 August 1635.

14. India Office Library and Records (IOL), G 36/105 fols 52–3, Richard Palmer to President, East India Company, 8 August 1670.

15. IOL E/3/31 no. 3462, Thomas Rolt to the Company, 21 August 1670.

16. Thomas Birch, *A Collection of the State Papers of John Thurloe*, (London, 1742), III, 386.

17. Birch, *Thurloe*, III, 173, 601.

18. PRO, SP 91/3 fols 56r–7v, affidavit of Henry Twentyman,

15 August 1640; Cambridge University Library, Additional Manuscripts 3924, Tsar Alexis's Credential Letter for Hebdon, February 1652.

19. PRO, SP 91/3 fols 114r–15v, letter from William Parker, 25 June 1666; wills of John Hebdon, Thomas Hebdon and Mary Hebdon are all preserved in PROB 11/333, section 77, and PROB 11/363, sections 1–3.

20. PRO, SP 29/42 fols 32–3, SP 29/50 fols 37I and 37II, accounts of purchases by Bryan 1661–2; T 51/10 fol 12–13, Navy Office about Bryan's purchase, 1661.

21. *Dopolneniya k aktam istoricheskim* (St Petersburg, 1855), V, 196.

22. PRO, T 51/10 fols 12–13.

23. PRO, PRO 22/60 no. 86, Charles II to Alexis, 29 December 1665.

24. PRO, PRO 22/60 nos 81, 82, 83, 84.

25. Bodleian Library, Clarendon MSS, vol. 81, fols 122–4.

26. Gordon, *Diary*, pp. 55–6.

27. *Sobranie gosudarstvennykh gramot i dogovorov* (Moscow, 1828), IV, 204–5. *Dopolneniya*, X, 471–3. See the entry on Bryan in *Russkii biograficheskii slovar'*, edited by A. A. Polovtsov (St Petersburg, 1908), p. 343.

28. PRO, SP 102/49 no. 15, Michael to Charles I, 19 December 1626; SP 91/2 fols 124r–v, ditto; Bodleian MSS Add. D75, fols 3v–4r, safe conduct 1626.

29. Gordon, *Diary*, pp. 57–104; Konovalov, 'England and Russia: Two Missions, 1666–1668', pp. 47–50.

30. For a full discussion see Charykov, *Posol'stvo ... Pavla Meneziya, passim*.

31. James Grant, *The Scottish Soldiers of Fortune* (London, 1889), p. iii.

32. BL, Harleian MSS 2149, fols 138–9.

33. Dukes, 'The Leslie Family', pp. 405–8.

34. PRO, SP 91/2 fols 152r–5v, Michael to Charles I, 29 January 1631; SP 91/2 fols 212r–v, Charles I to Michael, 26 February 1631/2; PRO 22/60 no. 58, Charles I to Michael, 12 August 1632.

35. PRO, PC 2/42 fol. 44; PC 2/42 fol. 48, PC 2/42 fol. 175.

36. Corporation of Gloucester, Letterbook (Stevenson 1420/1540), pp. 182–6.

37. Scottish Record Office, PC 11/5A no. 18.

38. PRO, E 157/15 fols 64r, 75r; E 157/16 fols 43r, 48r–v, 49r; all Licences to Pass Beyond the Sea, issued in 1631–2.

39. *HMC 9th Report*, pp. 234–7.

40. PRO, PRO 22/60 no. 28, James I to Michael, 20 May 1622.

41. PRO, SP 102/49–12, Michael to James I, 27 April 1623; SP 91/2 fols 89r–90v.

42. PRO, SP 16/66 fol. 66, Secretary John Coke to Calvert, 1627.

43. PRO, PRO 22/60–37, Charles I to Michael, 20 April 1629.

44. A. S. Mulyukin, *Priezd inostrantsev v moskovskoe gosudarstvo* (St Petersburg, 1909), pp. 157–9.

45. D. Tsvetaev, *Protestantstvo i protestanty v Rossii* (Moscow, 1890), p. 417.

46. The paragraphs concerning Ann Barnseley and Frances Rose were first printed in my article 'Britons in Russia, 1613–82', *Societas*, 7, no. 1 (Winter 1977), 19–46. They are reprinted with the kind permission of the editors.

47. Adam Olearius, *The Voyages and Travells of the Ambassadors sent by Frederick, Duke of Holstein, to the Great Duke of Muscovy, and the King of Persia* (London, 1662), pp. 131–2.

48. Nicholai Bantysh-Kamenskii, *Obzor vneshnikh snoshenii Rossii (do 1800 god)*, part 1 (Moscow, 1894), p. 111.

49. PRO, PRO 102/49 no. 37, Michael to Charles I, 7 March 1638; contemporary translation in *HMC Cowper*, II, pp. 177–9.

50. PRO, SP 91/3 fols 39r–40v, Digby to Sir John Coke, 4 September 1638.

51. PRO, SP 91/3 fols 49r–50v, John Cartwright to Coke, 20 May 1639; SP 91/3 fols 76r–v, petition for Ann Barnseley, *c.* 1638.

52. PRO, PRO 31/8/198/505 fol. 6, Digby MSS no. 113, Digby to Cartwright, 1 April 1629.

53. Olearius, *Voyages*, p. 132.

54. Tsvetaev, *Protestantstvo*, p. 511.

55. PRO, SP 91/3 fols 310r–v, petition of Frances Rose, *c.* 1661.

56. PRO, PRO 22/60 no. 78, Charles II to Alexis, 10 May 1661.

57. Tsvetaev, *Protestantstvo*, p. 413.

58. PRO, SP 29/441 fols 134, 135, Jacob Melosky's petition to

King, petition to Lord Arlington, *c*. 1673.
59.   PRO, SP 80/9 fols 8r–9v.
60.   PRO, PRO 22/60 no. 85, Charles II to Alexis, 12 April
      1665; SP 91/3 fols 342r–3v; PC 2/67 fol. 143; PC 2/68 fol.
      240; PC 2/69 fol. 420.

Aberdeen and North-East Scotland:
Some Archival and Other Sources

PAUL DUKES

Until the coming of the railway in the 1840s, north-east Scotland
was very much cut off from the rest of Britain, especially by the
overland route. Communication was somewhat easier by sea,
which also enabled ships sailing from Aberdeen and the other
ports to cross to the Low Countries and France, to Scandinavia
and the Baltic, almost as easily as they could get to some parts of
England and even Scotland. Evidence for these old connections
with Russia in particular is to be found in the archives of the
region, especially those of the University and the City.[1] Much
but not all of it has been published, and I would like to concentrate on what has not been published. But in order to place this
material in its context, I will have to refer to published sources; I
also want to make some mention of my search for evidence of a
non-written variety. Hence the title of the paper.

My approach will be basically chronological although, since we
will become involved in the complexities of family history, especially of the Leslies, the Gordons and the Keiths, a strict progres-
sion in time will not always be the most convenient. It will also be
necessary on occasion to broaden the focus from the basic
Russian subject of our attention to other parts of Europe, and
back to north-east Scotland especially.

We begin in the 1490s—1495 or 1496—with the ambassador
sent to Ivan III by King Christian I of Denmark who, according
to Herberstein, was attempting to secure the alliance of Muscovy
in a war against Sweden. This ambassador, sometimes referred
to as Master David, is identified by an historian of the early years

of the University of Copenhagen as 'Petrus Davidis de Scotia Aberdonensis'. It seems that Peter Davidson (the *filius* is understood) was first brought to Copenhagen in 1479 to help develop the new university. He was a Master of the Sorbonne, and must have left his native town well before the foundation of its first university, King's College, in 1494. There is no known record of him in Aberdeen itself.[2]

Just over half a century later, in 1556, north-east Scotland received its first known visitor from Russia, also an ambassador, Osip Nepea, sent by Ivan the Terrible with the returning expedition of Richard Chancellor. The account given by Hakluyt of Nepea's arrival makes it appear that the aims of the founder of King's College, Aberdeen, had as yet been little realized. Bishop Elphinstone had hoped that 'the ignorant would acquire knowledge and the rude erudition ... in the renowned ancient city of Aberdeen' in a 'remote portion of Scotland cut off from the rest of the kingdom by arms of the sea and very lofty mountains'.[3] Hakluyt tells us that after the shipwreck involving Nepea in the bay named 'Pettislego', just to the west of Fraserburgh, 'the noble personage of the sayde ambassadour with a few others (by Gods preservation and speciall favour) onely with much difficultie saved'. The account continues:

> In which shipwracke not onely the sayde ship was brokin, but also the masse and bodie of the goods laden in her, was by the rude and ravenous people of the countrey thereunto adjoyning, rifled, spoyled, and carried away, to the manifest losse and utter destruction of all the lading of the sayd ship. ...[4]

Unfortunately, again, there are no documentary records concerning this event in the archives of the region. Evidence of a different kind was provided on a visit to the site of the shipwreck, where some local oral tradition had designated two mounds at the fringe of the bay as 'the Russian graves'.[5] Some preparations were made towards carrying out a dig at the site, but the regional archaeologists advised against any amateur operations, even though the site was said to be in immediate danger of destruction. The 'Russian graves' or whatever they were soon succumbed to the bulldozer.

While Scots are known to have been in Muscovy in considerable numbers from about this time onwards, none of them car certainly be found to have specific connections with the north-east until we arrive at the Thirty Years War. In the so-called Swedish period of this war, several Scottish officers bearing the surname Leslie were involved, two of them with the first name Alexander. These have often been confused or incorrectly given a closer relationship than they in fact possessed. In his work on Gustavus Adolphus, Michael Roberts at first called the younger one senior and the elder one junior, and then identified them as one and the same.[6] B. F. Porshnev described the younger one as the father of the elder.[7] The younger one, born in 1582, is more easily identified as the later Earl of Leven prominent in the Civil War in Britain. The elder is described by the most authoritative genealogist of the Leslie family, Colonel Charles Leslie, KH, as the son of William Leslie of Creichie, a bastard line of Balquhain, near Inverurie. This Alexander is listed as father to two sons—John, a Lieutenant-Colonel, and Theodore; he is usually referred to as Sir Alexander Leslie of Auchintoul. However, the entry in *Registrum magni sigilli regum scotarum*, 1634–51, while duly noting the acquisition in 1637 of the estate of Auchintoul in Banffshire by one Alexander Leslie, knight, also lists as the knight's son (on page 232) one Gustavus. Now, according to Colonel Charles Leslie, the genealogist, the Earl of Leven had a son named Gustavus.[8] Could it be that it was the other Alexander Leslie who acquired the estate of Auchintoul rather than this one, on whose behalf Charles I wrote a letter of recommendation to Tsar Michael dated 7 March 1637? Certainly, this Leslie returned to Muscovy at some point in the late 1630s or 1640s after suffering disgrace during the War for Smolensk of 1632–4, and died in or around 1661 at the age of over ninety.[9]

Fellow historians above all must heed the advice of Professor Gordon Donaldson, Scottish Historiographer Royal, who warns against the assumption of consanguinity on the basis of identity of surname.[10] Possibly, then, the two Alexander Leslies were not related at all. Our problem of sorting them out is compounded by the observation of Colonel Leslie the genealogist that contemporaneous with Alexander Leslie in Muscovy were three colonels, several captains and other inferior officers of the name of Leslie.[11] Using the Colonel's published work and other unpublished genealogies in the University of Aberdeen archives, I have been able so far to identify tentatively just four of these other Leslies:

1. John of Balquhain who, because of debts, went to Germany, then to Muscovy, where he was made Colonel of Horse, and was killed on 30 or 31 August 1655 in storming a castle called 'Igolnith' or Igolwitz'.
2. Another Alexander, this time of Edinvillie or Edenville, who went to Muscovy and died without issue, on an unspecified date.
3. The Laird of Wardis or Wardhouse, possibly Sir John, who after his return from Muscovy on some unspecified date in the seventeeth century, died unmarried.
4. James, who 'was a Collonel in Muscovy and there behaved himself with great courage and conduct receiving many glorious wounds in the wars' and 'was come of the family of Aikenway. He was commonly called the King of Love but who were his parents is unknown'.[12]

James Leslie's nickname implies the probability of progeny, but none is listed. Certainly, Leslies lived on in Russia after the seventeenth century. Dr John Cook, in his *Voyages and Travels through the Russian Empire*, published in Edinburgh in 1768, mentions in 1737 a General Leslie, 'a gentleman of Scots extraction', who with his troops refused to surrender to the Tatars, and died like men.[13] Possibly, this was the Leslie listed as a signatory of the projects drawn up by the nobility in 1730.[14] There is, in the Aberdeen University Archive, an intriguing letter dated 26 January 1894 written by an Archibald Leslie of Kirinnie, Dufftown, to a Dear Sir identified only as somebody working on a book involving the Leslie pedigree. This letter includes the following passage:

> ... While at Malta I was engaged in a somewhat interesting correspondence with a branch of the Aikenway or Achintoul Leslies (I think) who have long been settled in Russia. The present head of that branch—James Leslie—holds a patent of nobility in Russia. He has recently built a church dedicated to the memory of the founder of the race of the name— Count Leslie's letters to me (written in French) and his pedigree are interesting documents. He obtained his estate in

Russia—or rather his forbears did, in the 1654 from Tzar Alexis. I have many documents connected with all the Leslie branches. ...[15]

Unfortunately, I have not been able to trace these documents, nor follow up any of the other leads suggested in the letter. 1654 appears to be too late a date for the award of an estate to Alexander Leslie, or at least for the first such award, since it is two years after the giving of presents to this Leslie and his wife on their turning Orthodox after, at least according to Olearius, the wife had offended the peasants on the Leslie estate near the Volga by throwing an icon on the fire, as a consequence of which the Leslies had decided to take up Russian nationality with the necessary additional abandonment of their previous Protestantism.[16]

The russified Leslies have made their mark in publication. In the catalogue of the Lenin Library in Moscow, I came across the following items: Alisa Lesli, *Davnishnee, nedavnee i tepereshnee* (Kiev, 1867); S. R. Lesli, *Predki: stseny iz proshlogo* (St Petersburg, 1902). For all the implications of the titles, there is nothing specifically Scottish in the first work, a collection of poems about childhood and other themes, nor in the second, a play set in the 1820s.

However, in an historical work, I. P. Lesli, *Smolenskoe dvorianskoe opolchenie 1812 goda* (Smolensk, 1912), there is a listing of Sergei Ivanovich Lesli, '*smolenskii gubernskii predvoditel' dvoryanstva*' (Smolensk guberniya marshal of the nobility). Coming down to the Soviet period, in keeping with the spirit of the age, perhaps, there is V. Lesli, *Ispol'zovanie stankov s programnym upravleniem* (Moscow, 1976). But proof that the Leslis are still alive and living in or near Smolensk, of which Alexander was governor over 300 years ago, was handed to me on a visit to Moscow in 1980 in the shape of a typewritten paper entitled 'Chastnaya perepiska sem'i Lesli i vneshnyaya politika Rossii v seredine XVII v'. This paper, now published,[17] gives interesting information about Alexander Leslie, for example, suggesting that his second arrival in Muscovy was in 1647, and describing complaints sent to him about his conversion to Orthodoxy in 1652 from fellow Scots in Sweden. The donor of the paper also informed me that he himself had talked to members of the Lesli family in or near Smolensk.

As we turn from Leslies to another family from north-east Scotland we have not finished with evidence for survival in the USSR. But we will return to latter-day Gordons after some remarks about their ancestors in the seventeenth and eighteenth centuries, especially the renowned Patrick, or Petr Ivanovich as he became known although never abandoning his staunch Roman Catholicism. The surviving portions of his diary are, as everybody knows, an outstanding source, while his contributions to the early education of Peter the Great and the military successes of Muscovy were immense. Through the use of archives in north-east Scotland, I have been able to take at least a little further the work of the late Professor Konovalov in supplementing the diary and filling its gaps. I should point out immediately that my work has been made much easier through the earlier labours of J. M. Bulloch, historian of the Gordon family as well as Fleet Street editor. It is from his papers that the following material has been taken. There are two letters to the Earl of Lauderdale, Secretary of State for Scotland residing in Highgate. The first, dated 16/26 September 1666, excuses his delay in Bruges *en route* for London, blaming it on the dilatoriness of a Captain Hill. The letter begins as follows:

Right Honorable,
    Fame, the divulger of great men's actions, hath not left the cold climate of Russia unsatisfyed or ignorant of the great favor and patronage yo'r L is pleased to affoord to our countreymen at the Court of his Royal Majesty upon occasion: in confidence whereof, I (being not only a stranger to yo'r L but to my owne native countrey in a manner) have presumed to make my advantages to yo'r L upon an emergency of the following quality.
    I shall omitt a relation of the reasons and necessities that drove me as well as many others, about the latter end of our intestine warre, from my native soyle to seek my fortune abroad, as likewise a progresse of my lyfe in the service of severall Princes hitherto untill I shall have the honor to kisse yor L hands myself.
    Be pleased then Most Noble Lord to know that I serve at present his Tzarsky Matie of Russia in the quality of a

Colonnell of horse, and am now employed in effaires as Envoy from his Tz. M. to his R. m. ... [18]

After that mission was over, Gordon wrote again to Lauderdale from Moscow on 15 July (probably NS) 1668:

Right Honorable,
    Though from the almost Frozen Zone yet with a most Torrid Affection ushered to my humble duty, I send thes addresses to your Lap. All humane actions, constitutions, complexions, and all terrestriall Creatures, yea even vegetives being tyed, and owing a sort of duty to the Celestiall Creatures, by reason of their influence upon them, even so wee who crawle in the lower Orbs cannot be but sensible of the duty wee should carry for those persons and spirits that move in higher Spheares. The many undeserved favours yor L was pleased to conferr upon me while I was in England, have put ane inviolable ty and engagement upon all my faculties. I am ignorant only of the meanes, and want sufficient ability, to give evident testimonies of my reall professions. ... I send by this occasion to your L a piece of unsophisticated Cavear in its Mothers Skine which will make a cup of good liquor tast the better, and hath besides an extraordinary strengthening quality, if ther be any thing which this Contrey affoords and may be usefull to your L Let me know your will, and it shall be duely fullfilled; but lest I prove tedious, with the tender of my most humble respects to your L most honorable Lady and Family I take leave continuing
    Right Noble Your L most faithfull & humble servant
    P. Gordon[19]

This second letter comes from the greatest gap in the diary, from June 1667 to January 1677. Proof that Gordon was back in Scotland in 1670 has been provided by the city records. These tell us that on 6 May 1670 Patrick Gordon, 'sub Imperio Serenissimi et Illustrissimi Imperatoris Russiae Magni', and his servant, Alexander Lumsden, were made honorary burgesses.[20] In order to answer some other questions about Patrick Gordon, we have to leave archives for other kinds of evidence. For example, in his diary there is a reference to the fact that in the year 1646 his father made one of his several moves to an estate which is left blank in the published version, probably because it was too much even for the conscientious German editor and translator Dr Posselt. In the original kept in Moscow, it is written 'Lony Focks', or 'Stony Focks' or indeed in some other way, since so far, after some scrutiny of maps and visits to the general area of Gordon's childhood, I have been unable to locate it. The same goes for the spot where Gordon said he would like to be buried, and the site of his birthplace, the old house of Auchleuchries, which according to page 231 of John B. Pratt's *Buchan* published in Edinburgh in 1858 'stands on a gentle eminence on the left bank of the burn. It is sheltered by the higher grounds on the north, and backed by plantations of wood'. It has now disappeared, possibly being built over by a newer farm house which has an unusually ceremonial entrance gateway with stone pillars.

To return to J. M. Bulloch's industrious researches, he continued these by enquiries concerning Posselt's German edition of the diary, including a letter to one Frederick Rennet in St Petersburg, who sent a reply from Moika 42 on 5 June 1912, including the following passage:

> Also by the way, I see in today's Russian paper that Professor Gordon, of Kharkoff University, has just been appointed Professor of Commercial Law in St Petersburg University. Perhaps he may have some research knowledge of the clan. I mention him because men of his position are much more likely to be useful than trying at government sources. Some years ago you wrote to me about Gordons now in the Russian army and at the war with Japan and I tried their War Office sources but always got stalled off with promises or the names of other offices to enquire at until the war was done and they still had nothing. Indexing and reference work don't exist here at all as you have it in England. That's why I suggest that this Professor Gordon may have better inside information.[21]

The Professor of Commercial Law may, of course, not have been of the clan Gordon at all since the Russian bearers of the name were often, as in *Doctor Zhivago*, Jewish.[22] Here is another subject investigated by the indefatigable J. M. Bulloch, who received a letter on it dated 1 March 1898 from a Joseph Jacobs of Acton. Mr Jacobs said that the Jewish 'Gordon' came from 'Grodno', adding the explanation that 'Hebrew like all Semitic

languages does not admit of double consonants, so that the
Hebrew name of the town is Gordon'. This subject was taken
further in 1921 in the pages of the *Aberdeen Free Press* and the
Jewish World. Bulloch wrote a letter to the first of these journals
on 9 February pointing out that the Lithuanian Jewish writer
Leon Gordon had written that his father had taken the name
from his mother's side after the Russian government had
ordered every Jew in 1818 to adopt a family name. On 16
February, the *Jewish World* reprinted this letter, adding the
comment that the Yiddish playwright Jacob Gordon came from
Mirgorod, which perhaps had given him the name Mirgordin
which then became Gordin and Gordon. On 2 March, the *Jewish
World* published another letter from J. M. Bulloch, who said that
he had heard from a friend in Philadelphia that: 'Mr Mayer
Sulzberger, a distinguished judge of that city, is of opinion that
the use of Gordon by Russian Jews arose from the fact that Lord
George Gordon, the anti-Catholic rioter, became a Jew, and he
was regarded by Jews on the Continent as a Messiah'. The
newspaper made the comment that there was no evidence that
Lord George Gordon had ever been regarded as a messiah, that
the chief rabbi had refused him as a proselyte, and that he was
received only on the personal authority of a Rabbi Jacob of
Birmingham. A further letter to the *Aberdeen Free Press* on 24
October from J. M. Bulloch communicated the intelligence that
Dr Benjamin Lee Gordon of Philadelphia, a native of Lithuania,
had informed him that the Jewish Gordons came from Vil'na,
deriving their name from *gordost'*—pride, a distinction given to
them along with the privilege, later lapsed, to live anywhere in
the Russian Empire. A final cutting from the Bulloch collection,
unusually without date or source, pointed out that the *Jewish
Encyclopaedia*, volume 7, stated that Stanislaus Poniatowski, himself descended from the Gordons, granted the Jews right of
residence in Kovno. W. M. Voynich, the well-known Polish
bookseller, had argued that the Jews had taken this name from
an old Scottish family, although some years later 'the head of the
house protested against the Hebraic annexation of the name'.[23]

The unresolved question of how the Jewish Gordons got their
name makes it difficult for us to know whether or not nineteenth-
and twentieth-century Gordons have been of Jewish or Scottish
origin. When, for example, we turn to another brief news item

from the *Aberdeen Free Press* on 6 March 1919, which referred to an item in the *Petrogradskaya Pravda* telling of resolutions of the Communist Party branch in Staraya Rusa, fifty miles south of Novgorod, passed after a report given by a Comrade Gordon. However, we can be certain that Gordons of Scottish descent have lived in the Soviet Union. A Mr Igor K. Gordon, an émigré living in Concord, California, as well as suggesting that General Brusilov came from the Bruce family, has written of his own father, grandfather and great grandfather, who was Governor-General of Warsaw. These forebears in turn had passed down old traditions, the grandfather for example asking the father to give his word of honour as a Scottish Gordon that he would join the army. Photographs accompanying I. K. Gordon's correspondence demonstrate the proud military bearing of the stern patriarch who exacted the promise.[24]

To return to the founders of the family tradition in Russia, we must recall that there were Gordons before and after Patrick as well as others at the same time. Once again, the materials assiduously collected by Bulloch are of great importance in sorting them out and establishing relationships. It must be pointed out that, as with the Leslies, scholars have made glaring errors. For example, even Academician Alekseev, or possibly a collaborator, confused Patrick with his distant kinsman and later son-in-law Alexander. On page 65 of his *Russko-angliiskie literaturnye svyazi*, a picture of Alexander is presented as one of Patrick. And the index attributes Alexander Gordon's *History of Peter the Great* to Patrick. To establish relationships correctly not only answers the exacting demands of scholarship, it also helps us to understand the manner in which kinship assisted the development in Russia of networks of patronage and mutual assistance among the Scots living in Russia. Ties could of course be formed by identity of place of origin as well as by blood. For example, Paul Menzies came from an Aberdonian family several members of which were associated with Patrick Gordon at various stages of his career, the closeness made all the greater in this case by common adherence to Roman Catholicism. Paul Menzies makes a brief appearance in the so-called Propinquity Books in the Aberdeen District Archive. The only other reference in them to Russia concerns a member of another of the Scottish families from the north-east, one George Keith, who was 'certainly informit to be departit this lyff in Muscovia'.[25]

Keiths, like Gordons and Leslies, had served in Russia from the early seventeenth century onwards, but of course the most famous of them is James, brother to the tenth and last Earl Marischal, an hereditary office held by the Keiths since it was first granted by Robert the Bruce. The fifth Earl Marischal founded Aberdeen's second university, Marischal College, in 1593. James was born with more of a silver spoon in his mouth than all the other Scots from the north-east, and might have pursued a glittering career in Britain if it had not been for his involvement in the Jacobite expeditions of 1715 and 1719. This is not the place to describe a life as significant in its way as that of Alexander Leslie and Patrick Gordon, even if less of it was spent in Russia.[26] Archival sources concerning James Keith are sparse in his homeland, but there are a few letters by him or about him recently donated to the University of Aberdeen by his descendant the Earl of Kintore. Perhaps the most interesting of these letters is by Alexander Falconer giving an eye-witness account of one of Keith's missions in 1741, the letter being dated 27 November of that year and including the following passage:

I have been little in one place ever since General Kieth [sic] being ordered to accompany the Turkish Ambassador from the frontiers of Turkey to Perevolochna the first town of her Government in the Ukraine. The exchange was in the following manner, both haveing merched to their respective frontiers accompanied both by a numerous suite and the troupes of the two forsaid powers, encamped, where after settleing the ceremonial part, both came to their utmost limits where a tent was erected partly on the Russian and partly on the Turkish Dominions where the two commissaries viz General Keith and the Serasquier of Bender were set haveing on their right hand the two Ambassadors and after the removal of the difficulties of the exchange the two foresaid commissaries delivered them into each other's hand. I never saw such a set of peoples as the Turks being altogether a noisy rabble not only begging money of us every day but tearing the dishes of meat out of our servants' hands. Once I dined with some of their Bashaws who do not know the use of forks or knives but tear with their hands like ravenous beasts. On the contrary the Russian Officers extremely polite and splendide.

Falconer went on to say that 'Our general has been very bad of a Reumatisme occasioned by cold he got in that expedition but I thank God is pretty well recovered'.[27]

Health was among the reasons that Keith was to use for leaving Russian service later in the 1740s, but before then he was to perform further sevices and gain more rewards. For example, on 4 October 1742 he was granted an estate at Rannenburg in Livonia, 23 *gaky* in size, with all the *myzy* or farms thereupon included. All the inhabitants of the estate were to recognize Keith as their *pomeshchik*, and all the stewards were to obey him.[28] According to some correspondence copies from the Berlin State Library before the Second World War, Keith's rewards went as far as a proposal of marriage from the Empress Elizabeth, but Professor Cross has conclusively shown this correspondence to be largely, even completely, forged later in the eighteenth century by a young adventurer claiming distant relationship to Keith, John Drummond.[29]

On 4 March 1749, Keith described his own primary reasons for leaving Russia in a letter to his kinsman John, the third Earl of Kintore, noting:

> ... the occasion of renewing a correspondence which had been too long interrupted, but the ridiculous jealosy of those where I then served made a crime to me of the most innocent letters I could write so far that I could hardly ever get one even from my brother or be allowed to write him, this with such coldness of the minister [Bestuzhev] to me at my return from Sweden, and the refusal to allow my brother to pass the rest of his days with me in Russia made me take the resolution of quitting a country where I had so many instances that the displeasure of a first minister was a capital crime and punished perhaps more rigorously than a real crime would be against the Souverain. I have reason to believe my countryman Ld Hyndford did not lessen the misunderstanding betwixt the minister and me for which I sincerely thank him, since by that he forced me to leave a country dangerous to all foreigners, and where innocence is no security against punishment, and to change masters very much to my advantage. ...'[30]

The departure from Russia of Keith brings to an end the most significant era of mercenary activity from north-east Scotland which accompanied the transition of Russia from embattled Muscovy to self-assertive empire. Many subjects of some interest are connected with the period from 1630 to 1750. Beyond those already touched on, there are those of freemasonry and Jacobitism. There are sources on these two subjects as yet unexplored and perhaps unexplorable in Aberdeen and its hinterland. In the second connection, the rich MacBean Collection of Jacobite pamphlets and other materials should be mentioned.[31]

There are still soldiers and sailors from north-east Scotland entering Russian service in the later eighteenth century. The Aberdonian representatives of the Scottish Enlightenment make some mention of Russia in their political writings.[32] There are a certain amount of unpublished nineteenth-century travel descriptions, for example that of Robert Wilson MD.[33] A new kind of contact arises towards the end of the nineteenth century with the growth of the herring fishing industry, which gave rise, among other things, to a local saying reported to me as: 'If it's a klondyke year for herring, the tsar's servants will get one and a half herrings each'. But this saying may have been no more widespread than the much reported, but never, as far as I have been able to find out, implemented practice of herring entrepreneurs from north-east Scotland papering their walls after the Russian Revolution with worthless tsarist banknotes. By today, fishing contacts have been renewed, and oil contacts made, each activity no doubt adding to the sources that will have to be investigated in due course.

Notes

1. For generous assistance in the compilation of this paper I should like to thank Mr Colin McLaren and Dr Dorothy Johnston of the University Archive and Miss Judith Cripps of the City Archive.
2. Sheriff Aeneas Mackay in the Aberdeen University Magazine *Alma Mater*, 5 March 1890, quoted by William Keith Leask in *Musa Latina Aberdonensis*, edited by William Keith Leask, 3 vols (Aberdeen, 1892, 1895, 1910), III, xvi–xviii. Sheriff Aeneas Mackay cites Sigmund von Herberstein, *Rerum Moscoviticarum Commentarii* (Basiliae,

1571), p. 117; J. Hamel, *England and Russia* (London, 1854), pp. 58–61.

3. Revd Henry Cowan, 'Bishop William Elphinstone', in *Studies in the History and Development of the University of Aberdeen*, edited by P. J. Anderson (Aberdeen, 1906), pp. 9–10.

4. *The Discovery of Muscovy: From the Collections of Richard Hakluyt*, edited by H. Morley (London and New York, 1889), p. 109.

5. *The Christian Watt Papers*, edited by David Fraser (Edinburgh, 1983), p. 12, contains the following passage from a letter by 'Granny Lascelles':

    Proceedings of the court case which took place in the great hall of Pitsligo Castle, after the wreck of the Edward Bonaventure, the crew of which are buried west of Joseph Mather's croft, many Broadsea folk were listed among those charged, also the Laird of Pitsligo's own sons, all those papers were burned by the soldiers.

    However, doubts have been cast upon the authenticity of these *Papers*. See the *Fraserburgh Herald*, 2 and 9 September 1983.

6. Michael Roberts, *Gustavus Adolphus: A History of Sweden, 1611–1632*, 2 vols (London, 1958), II, 565; M. Roberts, *Gustavus Adolphus and the Rise of Sweden* (London, 1973), pp. 113, 149.

7. B. F. Porshnev, *Tridtsatiletnyaya voina i vstuplenie v nee Shvetsii i Moskovskogo gosudarstva* (Moscow, 1976), pp. 242–3.

8. *Historical Records of the Family of Leslie from 1067 to 1868–1869*, edited by Colonel Charles Leslie, 3 vols (Edinburgh, 1869), III, 363, 410.

9. Paul Dukes, 'The Leslie Family in the Swedish Period (1630–5) of the Thirty Years' War', *European Studies Review*, 12, no. 4 (October 1982), 417–18.

10. Gordon Donaldson, *Surnames and Ancestry in Scotland* (n.p., n.d.).

11. Leslie, *Historical Records*, III, 410.

12. Aberdeen University Archive (AUA), MS 805, fols 19, 50, 70, 149. MS 2493 is almost identical. See also Leslie, *Historical Records*, II, 148; III, 95, 290, 353.

13. Cited in Francis Steuart, *Scottish Influences in Russian History* (Glasgow, 1913), p. 115.

14. Alexander Yanov, 'The Drama of the Time of Troubles, 1725–30', *Canadian-American Slavic Studies*, 12, no. 1 (Spring 1978), 41, considers this Leslie to be the sole foreign signatory. But he was probably Russian, although of Scottish descent.

15. AUA, MS 2814/6/41.

16. See note 9.

17. I owe this information to Professor Walter Leitsch, of the Institut für Ost- und Südosteuropaforschung der Universität Wien, who lists the publication as B. N. Morozov, 'Chastnaya perepiska sem'i Lesli i vneshnyaya politika Rossii v seredine XVII v.', appearing in *Molodye obshchest-vovedy Moskvy—Leninskomu yubileyu* (Moscow, 1982), pp. 110–12. If that pagination is correct, the paper must have appeared in abbreviated form.

18. AUA, MS 3051/2/9. This letter may be seen in the original in British Library (BL), Add. MSS 23125, fol. 96.

19. AUA, MS 3051/1/2/9. For the original, see BL, Add. MS 23129, fol. 231.

20. *Miscellany of the New Spalding Club* (Aberdeen, 1908), II, 431–2.

21. AUA, MS 3051/2/14/6.

22. Professor Vladimir Mikhailovich Gordon (1871–1926) was almost certainly not Jewish. I owe information about him to Professor W. E. Butler of University College, London.

23. The discussion of Jewish Gordons from AUA, MS 3051/2/14/6.

24. AUA, MS 2888.

25. *Miscellany of the Spalding Club* (Aberdeen, 1852), V, 352, 340. There is little archival material on Paul Menzies. For a full collection of documents, see *Posol'stvo v Rim i sluzhba v Moskve Pavla Meneziya (1637–1694)*, edited by N. V. Charykov (St Petersburg, 1906).

26. There are two typescript biographies of James Keith in AUA, by Adrian Keith-Falconer and H. Godfrey, at MS 2707 and MS 3163 respectively.

27. AUA, MS 3064/B 198.

28. AUA, MS 3064/B 146.

29. See *Study Group on Eighteenth-Century Russia Newsletter*, 7 (1979), 9–11.
30. AUA, MS 3064/B 335.
31. *Aberdeen University Library MacBean Collection*, compiled by Mabel D. Allardyce (Aberdeen, 1949).
32. See Paul Dukes, 'Some Aberdonian Influences on the Early Russian Enlightenment', *Canadian-American Slavic Studies*, 13, no. 4 (Winter 1979), 437–9.
33. AUA, MS 425.
    A further useful source of information is the local press, in continuous existence since the mid-eighteenth century. See, for example, John Wright, 'An Aberdonian in Russia', *Aberdeen Free Press*, 18 May 1906.

Anglo-Russian Relations 1714–1750: a Note on Sources

JEREMY BLACK

Scholars of Anglo-Russian diplomatic relations in the first half of the eighteenth century have an excellent tool to hand, the reports of the British envoys in Russia published in the *Sbornik imperatorskago Russkago istoricheskago obshchestva* (*SIRIO*). The recent republication of this series in microfilm will only serve to increase reliance on these reports, which are also available in microfiche. Unfortunately, these reports have two major drawbacks. Firstly, the dispute between Peter the Great and George I produced an effective breakdown of formal diplomatic contacts for the period 1719–30. Secondly, British diplomatic representation in Russia in the succeeding decade was, with the exception of the mission of Lord Forbes, in St Petersburg from June 1733 until May 1734, a low calibre one. Thomas Ward, Consul-General 1728–30, and Minister Resident from May 1730 until his death in February 1731, was of little importance, while Claudius Rondeau, Consul-General 1730–1, Minister Resident from September 1731 until his death in October 1739, was, despite his self-importance, insignificant. It was only the arrival in June 1740 of Edward Finch, MP, with the high rank of Envoy Extraordinary and Plenipotentiary, and a background of royal favour, diplomatic experience and the social and courtly skills that went with being a son of an earl, that altered the situation and ushered in a period of high-ranking diplomats such as Wych, Tyrawly and Hyndford.

As regards Hanoverian representation, George I was represented at first at St Petersburg by an envoy, Weber, but he also suffered from the 1719 breach. In common with the British Minister Resident, James Jefferyes, he retired to Danzig where he retained his character for a while. However, the resumption of Anglo-Russian diplomatic relations was not matched in the case of Hanover, and from the 1730s onwards Hanoverian interests, such as the import of Russian grain in the 1740s, were handled by British diplomats.

Thus in the 1720s and 1730s British diplomatic representation in Russia was on a low footing. Representatives received few instructions, and Russia received treatment little better than Denmark or Piedmont-Sardinia. The problem was compounded by that of the Russian representation in London. Affected by the 1719 rupture of diplomatic relations, Russian representation was restored only by Prince Cantemir of Moldavia, who reached London in March 1732. Cantemir, an intellectual of some weight, a characteristic he shared with other contemporary diplomats such as Canale and Horatio Walpole, enjoys a good reputation with historians on the strength of his cultural interests, and he possessed a high contemporary reputation for the same reason. The French Ambassador in Constantinople, the Marquis de Villeneuve, wrote in 1735, 'Le goût du Prince de Moldavie pour les lettres est comme héréditaire dans sa famille'.[1] This was not the same as diplomatic ability, however, and while he received some praise from the British ministry,[2] many doubted that he was suitable. In April 1732, Thomas Robinson, British Envoy in Vienna, mentioned Cantemir to the Austrian minister Prince Eugene 'as an extry person and one, who, as I had heard, was of as little merit as ever came out of Muscovy'. The following year, Count Biron, the Tsarina's favourite, told Rondeau that 'as he was a young man they could not well depend on his accounts', while the following year the well-informed Saxon envoy in London, De Löss, reported, 'Le Prince Cantimir tout bien intentionné qu'il est d'ailleurs, n'a pas assez d'expérience dans les affaires, et n'est pas avant dans la confidence du Ministère Anglais'.[3] Cantemir's political leanings also created difficulties. Though he was regarded by the French as an Anglophile, and himself expressed pro-Walpolite views, he lost the confidence of the British ministry. Horatio Walpole believed that he had been converted to pro-French views in 1736.[4]

Given the nature of British and Russian representation in St Petersburg and London respectively, it is not surprising that much contact between the two states occurred elsewhere. It is the intention of this paper to draw attention both to these contacts, and to source material, largely unutilized, available for the study of Anglo-Russian relations. It is important to note that the papers in the Public Record Office do not present enormous untapped source material for the history of Russia in this period, as for example do the reports of Brunswick diplomats held in the Staatsarchiv in Wolfenbüttel, which reflect a close interest in Russian politics associated with the marriage of Anton-Ulrich of Brunswick-Bevern to Anne of Mecklenburg, the mother of Ivan VI. However, there has survived much that is of great importance, particularly for Russian foreign policy.

This situation is not unique for Britain. In Vienna the Haus-, Hof- and Staatsarchiv contains, besides the official reports of the Austrian envoys in Russia, their private correspondence with Prince Eugene, held in the series Grosse Korrespondenz. In Paris, besides the reports of French envoys held at the Quai d'Orsay, there are also in the Archives de la Marine, currently held in the Archives Nationales, valuable reports from French consular officials in Baltic ports, in particular St Petersburg. There is much useful material on Franco-Russian trade and on schemes to develop it; the series is B7, Pays Etrangères. Furthermore, much light is cast on Russian policy in the Baltic by French consular reports in this series from Danzig and Hamburg. Some of those from Danzig have been printed, in French, with a Polish translation, by the Polish historian Edmund Ciéslak. Particularly valuable are those from Mathy, Consul in the late 1710s. While considering foreign sources it is also useful to note two printed, but underused, sources: E. Herrmann, *Diplomatische Beiträge zur Russischen Geschichte aus dem königlich sächsischen Hauptstaatsarchiv zu Dresden 1728–34* (St Petersburg, 1870); Duque de Liria, *Diario del viaje a Moscovia del Duque de Liria y Xerica* (Madrid, 1889). Hermann's volume reflects, but in no way exhausts, the rich material for Russian history in the Saxon diplomatic archives. James Fitzjames Stuart, Duke of Liria, was the son of James II of England's bastard, the Duke of Berwick. While his father was a French marshal and his first cousin, Earl Waldegrave, British Ambassador Extra-

ordinary and Plenipotentiary in Vienna, Liria was Spanish
Ambassador and Minister Plenipotentiary in Russia. He arrived
in September 1727, leaving in November 1730, and his diary is a
most valuable source.[5]

There is little material on Anglo-Russian relations in this
period in British archives, other than those in the Public Record
Office and the British Library. The correspondence of Lord
Glenorchy (and his wife), during the latter's posting as Envoy
Extraordinary in Copenhagen in the 1720s, contains material on
the Danish response to the Russian threat. They are held in
Bedford, in the Lucas papers in the Bedfordshire Record
Office. Lady Lucas freely grants permission to consult them.
The Trevor papers in the Buckinghamshire Record Office in
Aylesbury contain some interesting letters from British envoys
in St Petersburg, in the early 1740s, particularly from Edward
Finch. Finch's papers in the Leicestershire Record Office are
very disappointing. The Waldegrave papers at Chewton Hall,
Chewton Mendip, contain very little, though there are a few
letters from Liria. The papers of James, Viscount Stanhope, in
the Chevening deposit at the Kent Archives Office in Maidstone,
are disappointing for Anglo-Russian relations in the 1710s
though there is some interesting material for British foreign
policy in general. The Hotham papers in Hull University
Library contain the papers of Sir Charles Hotham, sent to Berlin
in 1730. He and his correspondents were greatly interested in
the impact of Russia's constitutional and political crisis of 1730
on Russian foreign policy. The Townshend papers in the
Norfolk Record Office in Norwich, contained in both the
Bradfer Lawrence and the Townshend collections, have little of
great importance for Anglo-Russian relations. Unfortunately
the remainder of Townshend's papers, held at Raynham,
contain nothing valuable that is not in print, whilst Horatio
Walpole's at Wolterton are closed to scholars.

The Bodleian Library contains the fascinating letterbook of
Weber, Hanoverian representative in St Petersburg in the late
1710s (the reference is MS Fr. d. 35). There is also Cantemir
material in the Zamboni papers in the Rawlinson Collection,
while the Dashwood papers contain the (already printed)
account of Sir Francis Dashwood's 1733 trip to Russia. Another
traveller whose account is in print, but underused, was John

Lindsay, twentieth Earl of Crawford (1702–49), who served in the Russian army against the Turks in 1738, and described his experiences in his memoirs, which were published in 1753.[6] The Stuart papers in Windsor Castle, for whose examination prior permission must be obtained, contain a wealth of material on European international relations in the period. These are of great interest for historians of Anglo-Russian relations when they reflect Jacobite attempts to gain Russian support. The letters of Admiral Gordon from St Petersburg are fairly well known, but it is also important to note that there is much material in the reports of the Jacobite envoys in Vienna. In the 1720s, in particular, Austria was probably the best informed about Russia of the major European states.

The remainder of this paper will be devoted to material in the State Papers series in the Public Record Office, and in the Department of Manuscripts, British Library. Much material of diplomatic interest is in the latter because the Additional Manuscripts series holds the papers of the Duke of Newcastle, Secretary of State for the Southern Department from 1724 to 1748, and then for the Northern Department until 1754. As relations with Russia fell under the care of the Northern Department it might be thought that Newcastle's papers for the 1720s do not contain any relevant material. This is not the case because Newcastle handled relations with France, and Paris, one of the leading diplomatic centres of Europe (in a way London never was), saw frequent contacts between British and Russian diplomats.

Furthermore, the volumes reflect British thinking about Russia. Thus in 1719 James Craggs the younger, Secretary of State for the Southern Department, wrote to Newcastle, then Lord Chamberlain, revealing that he, Newcastle, Stanhope and Lord Sunderland, the First Commissioner of the Treasury, were all in favour of using the British fleet in the Baltic to attack Russia:

> ... but Sr. Jn. Norris has in a manner protested against it. He has now 17 ships of line. I own to you he has surprised me, besides other reasons I thought his personal pique to the Czar and his envy to Byng would have spurred him on, but truly he comes out like all your Blusterers a very very wise man.

A week later he revealed the ministry's awareness of the vital relationship between Anglo-Russian relations and the ministry's parliamentary position, at a time when the opposition was exploiting the government's failure to solve the Baltic crisis, 'If Sr. Jn. Norris would be pleased to take ye Czar and destroy his fleet, I should not much fear his allys next sessions'.[7]

Four years later Newcastle's correspondence with Sir Robert Walpole reveals ministerial fear of Russia and the importance of Anglo-Russian relations. Walpole declared his support of an Anglo-Russian reconciliation, writing 'my politicks are in a narrow compasse, if we keep perfectly well with France and the Czar, I am under no apprehensions of foreign disturbances, which alone can confound us here'. Newcastle expounded the domino theory. Were Britain's Hessian protégé, Frederick I, to be replaced in Sweden by Peter I's protégé (soon to be his son-in-law), Charles Frederick Duke of Holstein-Gottorp, then Russia would not threaten Scotland, and seek to replace George I by the Jacobite James III:

> ... security is the first thing to be thought on, and if the D. of Holstein should be put in possession of the Crown of Sweden by the Czar, he must be upon all occasions subservient to and dependent upon him, this must naturally make the Czar Master of the Baltick, which is so near Scotland, that it will not be a difficult matter for him enterprising as he is. ... Our northern trade will be at his devotion, and I doubt when he has turned out one King he will think of doing the same to another especially the only one that can thwart his designs in that part of the world. But it is much easier to foresee these ill consequences than to prevent em. ... I think ... that it is possible by a sum of money to stir up the Northern Princes of Denmark Sweded [sic] and perhaps Prussia to oppose a power, which will certainly at last, if not timely be prevented be too strong ... I am heartily afraid of ye Czar.[8]

After Newcastle became Secretary of State in 1724 his papers contain much interesting material revealing Britain's developing attitude to Russia. In 1725 Horatio Walpole presents the death of Peter I as an opportunity to destroy the Holstein interest in Russia, to support Sweden against Russia and, if Peter II should succeed in Russia, to enable George I to become the most powerful ruler in northern Europe.[9] In 1727 Newcastle reflects that the Anglo-Swedish alliance has had the beneficial effect of preventing Russia sending troops to aid Austria against Hanover,[10] and the documents reveal an approach from Prince Kurakin, Russian Envoy in Paris, to Horatio Walpole for a reconciliation. Walpole informed Kurakin that, 'the differences between England and Russia were in a great measure personal with respect to the two sovereigns, and that those two sovereigns were now dead, ...'. There was a great degree of truth in this as no essential Russian interests were involved in Peter I's dynastic policies over Mecklenburg and Holstein-Gottorp, and the same was true for Britain and George I's Hanoverian interests. The British ministry responded to Kurakin's approach by stating that George II was 'very desirous of renewing the good correspondence with that Crown, ... and as to former differences, His Maty. thinks, if their intentions are sincere, they will readily agree that all that should be forgotten ...'. The attempt to improve relations failed—Catherine I was more concerned to preserve her Austrian alliance; the papers in the Newcastle collection are essential evidence for the attempt.[11]

Further evidence of a continued British interest in a reconciliation comes from the Newcastle papers for 1730. In July the British envoys in Paris were instructed to inform Count Golovkin that George II favoured a reconciliation and the exchange of ministers and that George II would not insist upon the Tsarina Anne—'abandoning the interest of the Duke of Mecklenburg', her brother-in-law, who was in conflict with George II, as Elector of Hanover. Two months later Waldegrave, now representative in Paris, was ordered to 'continue to assure Count Golofkin of His Majesty's readiness to come to a perfect reconciliation with the Court of Russia, on the foot mentioned in my former letters of forgetting on both sides all this is past, and sending Ministers to each other'.[12] Thus, the Newcastle papers contain material of direct importance for the history of Anglo-Russian relations. In addition they contain numerous references of interest to those studying Russian relations with other states as the following two examples show. In 1727 Benjamin Keene, Minister Plenipotentiary in Spain, recorded the Queen of Spain as saying, 'As to the Muscovites she said she believed they would fall into their ancient barbarity'. Eleven years later Waldegrave reported a conversation with the French premier ministre, Cardinal Fleury, on the Russo-Turkish war:

> The Cardinal did not conceal a pleasure at the accounts he had of the ill condition the Muscovites were in, not from his wishing well to the Turk, but from the probability of the Russians becoming a troublesome power, should the present Empress be succeeded by a warlike Prince.[13]

Other holdings in the British Library are of considerable value for the history of Anglo-Russian relations. The Coxe transcripts, prepared by Archdeacon William Coxe for his monumental work on the ministry of Sir Robert Walpole, contain Horatio Walpole's very valuable reflections on British foreign policy in the late 1730s including his scheme for a grand alliance of 1740. The Townshend papers contain some material; for example, there is an undated note from Townshend to George II, stating that Rondeau 'is only directed to sound, and not to transact anything there'.[14] More valuable are the Whitworth papers. Charles Whitworth had served in Russia in 1705–10 and 1712, and his dispatches and instructions for that period are preserved in the *SIRIO* collection. He maintained his informed interest in Russian affairs, during subsequent postings at The Hague, Berlin and the Congress of Cambray. His reflections on Anglo-Russian relations are always of great interest. In February 1723 he wrote to Sir Luke Schaub, Ambassador at Paris:

> Je ne voye pas même que le Roy aye la moindre chose à demeler avec le Czar pendant la Paix Generale; Il n'y a que cette malheureuse affaire de Mecklenbourg, qui nous inquiete de tems en tems, et encore est ce a tort; car le Czar ne s'hazardera point aux voyes de fait, pendant que tous les voisins sont armés et en repos: Tout ce qui est à craindre à present, est qu'il ne fatique tellement le Danemarc par des allarmes continuelles, et les depenses d'un armament naval chaque eté, qu'elle choisisse enfin de souscrire à quelque Traité désavantageux, plus tôt que d'y être toujours exposée.

In August 1723 he informed George Tilson, Under-Secretary of State in the Northern Department, that Britain, by displaying fear of Russia, only encouraged her, and stated that the real danger was a Franco-Russian alliance, 'the Czar if he lives may be *really* dangerous'. In November 1723 he informed Tilson of a conversation he had had with the elder Prince Kurakin:

Prince Kurakin has given me a very dismal account of the condition to which his poor country is reduc'd by the Czar's continual exactions: He says the expedition on the Caspian sea has cost prodigiously both in Men and Money; and that the Czar's officers finding the peasant unable to pay the Taxes have at last seiz'd their Horses and cattle in several Provinces, which puts them out of a condition of plowing their lands; and this he says has brought them so low, that he has been able to draw only a thousand Rubles this last year from his whole estate, which is none of the least considerable of the country. He seems persuaded that the Czar having no male issue, is grown very indolent as to the point of his succession, and does not care what becomes of it and his country when he is dead: His only ambition being now to get himself a name, and to keep up his reputation whilst he lives cost what it will; Pereunte me pereat Mundus.

He tells me a rupture with the Porte is unavoidable, and show'd me an article of their new treaty with the Sophy which seems directly levell'd against the Turks, and which known at Constantinople wou'd certainly put all into a flame; But that the Czar was very unconcern'd at it in hopes of recovering Asoph again, which he intends to besiege as soon as ever the war is declar'd; Thô that expedition is not like to be so easy, now the Turks have their hands at liberty on every side, as he found it in the former war, especially since the Russian Forces in the Ukraine are in a wretched condition. Prince Gallitzin who has been lately sent thither to take upon him the Command in Chief is extremely dissatisfied with the posture of their affairs, and has complain'd to his father-in-law Prince Kurakin, that they have neither Horses, Magazins, nor Money; and that the troops are ill disciplin'd and not fitt to take the field. I suppose the Czar's greatest relyance is on his Guards, who are seven thousand men and always march with him, and on his artillery. This account of his situation, which I am persuaded is real, may be worth some reflection, and tho' it has made a tedious letter may be of use in comparing notes with your other Northern correspondence; This and your Prussian Treaty may serve instead of Jesuits bark, to cure your spring agues.[15]

The various series in the Public Record Office are also of great value. The obvious sources for Anglo-Russian relations are State Papers, Foreign, but there is also a wealth of material in other series. Particularly important for the late 1710s and early 1720s is material on British naval expeditions to the Baltic, exploited well by David Aldridge in his unpublished London doctoral thesis of 1972, 'Sir John Norris and the British Naval Expeditions to the Baltic Sea, 1715–1727'. State Papers, Domestic, for which there is a printed catalogue, occasionally contains material. There is some material on Jacobite–Russian relations[16] and on fears about Russia supplying arms to British Jacobites in 1725, and occasional letters of some interest, such as one from Horatio Walpole in 1740 on his scheme for a grand alliance.[17]

There is very valuable material in the State Papers, Regencies series, which contains the correspondence between the minister, usually a secretary of state, though in 1736 Horatio Walpole, who accompanied the King to Hanover, and the Regency government in London. There is little of interest in some years, 1729 for example, but some years are of major importance. George I's visits have left much on Anglo-Russian relations in the volumes for his period, while in 1732 there is much concerning fears of a Prusso-Russian marriage, and in 1740 a large amount on Anglo-Russian negotiations.

The diplomatic intercepts (class SP 107) contain very few intercepts of Russian dispatches, but there is some very interesting material on how Anglo-Russian relations were perceived by other states. In 1733, when the Russian invasion of Poland led to the War of the Polish Succession, the Russians found it very difficult to dislodge Britain from her position of neutrality. Russian requests for the dispatch of a British fleet to the Baltic, to counter French naval moves, were refused, Britain refused to support actively the Russian-backed Saxon candidate for the Polish throne, and to widen her commercial negotiations with Russia to include a treaty for mutual guarantee of territory.[18] This appeared to be anti-Russian, though in fact it was in direct accordance with Britain's unwillingness to widen her treaty with Austria of 1731, the second Treaty of Vienna, to include Russia.

However, in contrast with the marked anti-Russian stance of British policy in 1720–1 and again for most of the late 1720s, British policy could be construed as pro-Russian and class SP 107 provides some evidence of this attitude. On 21 August 1733 Baron Sparre, Swedish Envoy in London, reported a conversation of the previous day with the Secretary of State for the Northern Department, Lord Harrington. Harrington informed Sparre of the Russian invasion aimed at thwarting the election of the French candidate, Stanislaus Leszczynski, and Sparre wrote:

> I could sufficiently observe by his discourse, that seeing King Stanislas's [*sic*] election could not be hindered otherwise, those advices were not unacceptable to the Court here; for he absolutely took the part of the Russians, saying ... that by a Treaty of 1717, Russia as Guarantee [*sic*] was obliged to maintain the Liberty of Poland, against all force and oppression, nor to permit King Stanislas [*sic*] to be chosen ... From this discourse of the Secretary of State as well as from divers others of his before, as also from other Intelligence I have here at Court, I am certain that the Court is now more in the Russian interest, than I ever suspected they would be. I will not accuse them, that they are so of inclination; but the Alliance with the Emperour [*sic*] and the safety of the King's German Dominions upon the foot of his present system, may be the true motives thereto.

Four days later Sparre reported that, although Harrington had disclaimed to him any pro-Russian tendencies, 'this Court believes they find their account by the Russian Court better now than they have done for these fourteen years past'.[19]

This material and similar reflections by Swedish diplomats which can be found throughout the series are of great importance. Anglo-Russian relations cannot be viewed in isolation: the British ministry viewed them in the context of general foreign policy, particularly in the Baltic, and, in specific terms, in relation to Sweden and, from the early 1730s increasingly, Prussia. A guarantee of Russian territory would have amounted in practice to a resumption of Peter I's diplomatic strategy of 1716, to committing Britain–Hanover and her subsidized allies, particularly

Denmark, to war against Sweden should she seek to regain her Baltic provinces. This was the issue that handicapped efforts to improve Anglo-Russian relations from 1725 until the 1740s. Britain sought to retain the alliance of Denmark and Sweden, both greatly concerned about the prospect of an Anglo-Russian reconciliation. Responding to Swedish fears of Anglo-Russian negotiations Newcastle had, in June 1728, given the assurance that 'no negotiation of this sort will be entered into by His Majesty without previously communicating it to the King of Sweden and Count Horn, and having their concurrence and approbation'. Four years later Harrington informed Walter Titley, Minister Resident in Copenhagen, that:

> ... the Draught of an act for including the Kings of Denmark, Sweden, and Prussia, with the Czarina and the Duke of Holstein in the late Treaty of Vienna have been transmitted hither, but as his Maty. has all along declared that he could not give any guaranty to Muscovy, it has been returned with an exception to the general guaranty stipulated in that Treaty. And Denmark may be assured that the King has no thoughts of doing anything as to that Inclusion which may be disagreeable to his old friends and allys.[20]

It is only when Anglo-Russian relations are securely placed within the foreign policies of the two states (Russia had to consider her relations with Austria and Prussia when negotiating with Britain) that a balanced picture can be achieved.

Turning to State Papers, Foreign, it is firstly important to note that Captain John Deane, sent to Russia as Consul-General in June 1725 but expelled the following month as he was really on secret political business, left an important account of his mission, that can be found outside the main State Papers, Russia, series, in State Papers, Russia, supplementary: the volume number is SP 91/107. Interesting material on Anglo-Russian relations in 1727–8 can be found in State Papers, United Provinces. Horatio Walpole produced a valuable summary of British policy in his memorandum of 1727, 'Considerations qui peuvent servir à donner quelque idée des Mesures préalables que les Alliés devroient concerter entre eux pour regler leur conduite au Congrès de Cambray'. He stated his view that there was no necessity for poor Anglo-Russian relations, and firmly placed these relations in the context of European affairs:

Il y avoit à la verité une grande froideur et mesintelligence entre le feu Roy d'Angleterre et le feu Czar et la Czarine, mais comme cela n'en vint pas à une rupture ouverte, it parut que c'etoit plutôt un Differend personel entre les Souverains respectifs, qu'une Querelle entre les deux Nations, et comme depuis ces Souverains sont morts, il ne paroit pas qu'il y ait de raison pourquoy leurs Differends ne seroient pas aussi finis, et on ne voit pas ce qui pourroit empecher le renouvellement de l'ancien commerce et bonne correspondance entre l'Angleterre et la Russie ... tout ce qui s'est passé, par raport aux affaires de l'Europe, principalement durant ces deux dernieres années, a clairement fait voir, qu'il y a une relation et une union inseparable entre les Puissances du Nord et du Sud; et que le feu Czar, ni la Czarine ... n'auroient formé aucune enterprise pour troubler la Tranquilité du Nord, si ce n'eût été en vertu des Traitez et Conventions qu'ils avoient faits avec L'Empereur et l'Espagne; et que tout succés, dont leurs Entreprises de ce côté là auroient été accompagnées, auroit été également avantageux à leurs Majestés Imple. et Catholique ....[21]

The same series contains interesting material on Russia forwarded from The Hague by the Earl of Chesterfield in 1728 and, four years later, Chesterfield's account of an approach for an alliance from the Russian Envoy, Count Golovkin.[22] An obvious source is State Papers, Sweden, but less obvious are the reports from Richard Sutton, Envoy Extraordinary to Brunswick-Wolfenbüttel and Hesse-Cassel in the period 1727–31, held in the patchy series State Papers, German States. It is unclear what the exact source of these reports was, presumably German diplomats in Russia, but it is interesting to note that this route was sometimes used by the press for information about Russia. The *St James' Evening Post* of 17 August 1728 carried a report from The Hague of 'some advices (by the way of Cassel)' mentioning the approaching fall of the principal German ministers in Russia. Russia played only a minor role at the two great, and unsuccessful, peace congresses of the 1720s, Cambray and Soissons, and reports from the British representatives there yield little. There is much of interest on Russo-Turkish relations in State Papers, Turkey, and the instructions to the British diplomats in Constantinople chart the change in British attitudes to Russia, from encouraging tension in the early 1720s to discouraging it a decade later.

State Papers, Germany (Emperor), contain much of value. From the negotiation of a treaty in 1726, the Russian alliance had been of great importance to Austria. Therefore Austria sought to improve relations after her reconciliation with Britain in 1731.[23] This was not an easy task, and the dispatches of Thomas Robinson throw much light on Anglo-Russian relations. Robinson himself was greatly in favour of improved relations, and his correspondence provides interesting evidence of a divergence in views about Anglo-Russian policy. In September 1732 he sent a secret letter to Newcastle that warned of the danger of France gaining Russia's alliance, and noted 'We have not, as we might have done, put ourselves upon such a footing in Muscovy as to have any credit there … '.[24] Robinson's letter criticized Harrington and the Hanoverian ministers, and by implication George II, for failing to gain Russian and Prussian friendship. There is much valuable material in the 1731–2 correspondence on Britain's opposition to the scheme for a marriage between Anne, Princess of Mecklenburg, the niece, and assumed heir, of Tsarina Anne, and a son, or nephew, of George II's rival, brother-in-law, and first cousin, Frederick William I of Prussia.[25] The British pressed the Austrians to block the marriage.[26] There is also interesting material on contacts in Vienna between Robinson and the Tsarina's favourite, and envoy, Count Levenwold.[27] The British concern over the marriage of Anne of Mecklenburg is a salutary reminder of the importance of dynastic factors, including unpredictable elements such as birth and death, in the international system of the period.

State Papers, Germany, also provides much evidence about the development of what could be termed Britain's Northern System, of vital importance for the development of Anglo-Russian relations. The accession of the Hanoverian dynasty had handicapped British foreign policy with the need to defend the most vulnerable Electorate against potential foes—Russia from the late 1710s until 1731, Austria in 1725–31, Prussia from 1726 and France from 1741. The improvement in Anglo-Russian relations in the mid-1730s solved, at least temporarily, this problem.

In 1733–5 Hanoverian relations with Prussia were very poor, with tension running high over conflicting interests in Mecklenburg in 1733–4, and Hamburg in 1735. The solution was clear, 'We need only let the Czarina loose upon him, and what will become of his Kingdom at least'.[28] The Austrian Chancellor, Count Sinzendorf, told Robinson that 'the Emperor, the King and the States General themselves could not have a better check upon the King of Prussia than the Russians, who, were it for that reason alone, would be worth the humouring'.[29] Russia was to be used to redress, in George II's favour, the German balance, upset by the rise of the Prussian army. This strategy, of using Russia to threaten Prussia, was basic to Anglo-Russian relations until 1756.

It should be noted that State Papers, Germany, does not only contain material of a diplomatic nature. In 1739 Robinson forwarded an anonymous 'Extrait d'une lettre de St Petersburg' which gave a view of Russian factions, the poor state of the Russian fleet, and the weakness of Russia. To quote just an extract of this interesting document:

> L'argent est aussi rare en Russie que le sçavoir, et la politesse. La pluspart des terres restent en friche depuis cinq ou 6 ans; Les habitants des provinces sur les frontieres se sont sauves par desespoir, chez les Voisins, temoin l'Ukraine, qui est presque deserte. Dans cet etate de foiblesse, une ou tout au plus, deux campagnes, feront tomber la Russie d'elle même, das une confusion, qui la jetteroit dans son premier Etat.[30]

Such claims were frequent: few could appreciate the strengths of Russia, and many seem disinclined to accept that the European system had been permanently altered by her rise.

Three further important series should be mentioned. There is a mass of material on Anglo-Russian relations in State Papers, Prussia. Particularly, during the mid-1720s, when, in 1723–6, Anglo-Prussian relations were very good and there were no Anglo-Russian diplomatic relations, Britain relied on her envoys in Berlin to supply information on Russian developments. Aside from information on Russian developments, and Anglo-Russian relations, there are also occasional glimpses of the attitudes of British diplomats. In 1720 Whitworth wrote, 'the Czar continues to treat the poor Swedes with all the arrogance of an entire and barbarous conqueror. A great part of Europe are like to feel his humour by degrees'. Five years later Townshend rejected an idea of Colonel Du Bourgay, Envoy Extraordinary in Berlin, that Britain should support the 'Old Russ' faction in the struggles in St Petersburg, and urged a firm stance towards Russia, 'It is in vain to think of anything real and fair from the Court of Muscovy to our purpose, they never meant honestly in regard to the King, and they are now gone entirely into another interest, and are pursuing with eagerness a quite different scheme'.[31]

A major source that has been unused is that of State Papers, Hamburg. Hamburg was a major trading centre with close commercial links with Russia. Many reports on Russian affairs that appeared in British newspapers were derived from Hamburg newspapers. However, it was not this that makes the series so important. Rather it was the bustling, self-important figure of Sir Cyril Wych, who represented Britain in the Hanse towns from 1713 until 1741 when he was posted to Russia, where he served from 1742 until 1744. Wych was of importance because he had very close links with the court of Holstein-Gottorp, which was then in Russia. In seeking appointment as British Envoy to Russia in 1725 he argued, 'je crois que les etroites liaisons que j'ai eu autrefois avec le Duc d'Holstein et la bonte dont il m'a toujours honoré me procureroit des certains facilites ... je connois tous les Ministres de cette Cour, et que je puis me flater d'etre asses bien dans l'esprit du Duc d'Holstein'. In 1728 Horatio Walpole wrote 'he has always seem'd to be a Holsteiner to me', and in 1741 the Russian diplomat Bestuzhev complained of his attachment to the House of Holstein. In 1735 the British government gave him permission to accept the Duke of Holstein's offer of the Order of St Anne.[32] It is clear that much of Wych's information derived from the Holstein connection,[33] and this makes his reports particularly valuable, as British diplomats in Russia, such as Rondeau, tended to have poor relations with the Holstein court, while British diplomats who considered Russian affairs tended to hope for the success in the factional battles within Russia, neither of the Holsteiners, nor of other ministers with a German background, such as Ostermann, but of the 'Old Russ'.

The third series that is of importance, in particular for the 1720s, is State Papers, Saxony-Poland. Saxony-Poland played a major role in British attempts to create an anti-Russian alliance. Furthermore, there are interesting accounts of meetings with Russian diplomats,[34] reflections on Anglo-Russian relations and reports on Russian developments. On 21 March 1725 Finch reported discontent in Russia, a decaying fleet and an unpaid army. The following month he wrote to Townshend that, 'they generally think here, that the Czarine [*sic*] will not be able to maintain herself on the Throne, at least with that Tranquility which she wishes; the Generality of the Muscovites can not conceal the Inclination they have for the Czarowitz'.

Townshend's instructions to Finch in 1725 provide some very interesting information on the development of British attitudes to Russia, in a very crucial year of Anglo-Russian diplomacy. In March he had been unsure 'whether the Czarina can establish her authority', but by September it was clear that Catherine I would not fall speedily. Finch was told to approach the Russian envoy, Prince Dolgorukii, and:

> . . . as we take him to be an Old Russ, and of that party that is for the true good of his Country; you might further intimate that England and Russia have been always well together, that their real interests should naturally unite them closer; and that no Nation can be so useful to the Muscovites as the English in preserving their new acquisitions, and in all points of Trade and Commerce; and that the Reconciliation between the King and the Czarina, and the alliance between them and France, sticks solely upon a point that concerns only the interests of strangers, the pretensions of the Duke of Holstein, and in no wise regards the welfare of Muscovy which is more immediately concerned in the speedy conclusion of that Treaty. If you find this Prince Dolhorucki a true hearted Old Russ, and consequently no partisan of the Holstein Faction, you will endeavour to make all the use of him you can to insinuate to his Court his Maty's Desire of the Czarina's friendship, in the promoting of which he may do a signal service to his country and prevent its suffering for the sake of Foreigners. If he falls into this our way of thinking and talking, and you find you can open yourself to him, I will instruct you in all points relating to the Reconciliation and Allyance, which perhaps you may by his means advance more effectually than we can by any one at Petersbourg itself.

The approach led nowhere. Though Dolgorukii told Finch that there were no lasting reasons why the two countries should not be friends, he did not give Finch an opportunity to make the approach detailed above, and chose to talk about 'English horses' and other such topics. By October Townshend had changed his mind and Finch was instructed not to discuss a potential alliance.[35]

Episodes such as this reveal how much can be gained by scholars of Anglo-Russian relations through looking in series other than State Papers, Russia. There is still much work to be done on evidence for Anglo-Russian contacts in these series, while work needs also to be done on the private papers of British diplomats. It is particularly to be hoped that Raynham and Wolterton papers will be opened to scholars. Furthermore, it is probable that European archives will reveal material on Anglo-Russian relations. The Hannover Hauptstaatsarchiv contains some very interesting correspondence, for the latter years of the War of the Austrian Succession, between the Hanoverian government and the Earl of Hyndford, Minister Plenipotentiary, and then Ambassador Extraordinary and Plenipotentiary, in St Petersburg, 1744–9. They show that he maintained a secret correspondence with George II, via the Hanoverian government and the Hanoverian Chancery in London, a correspondence that the British ministry knew nothing about. This *secret du roi* sought to pitch Russia against Prussia at a time when the British ministry sought to join the two in an alliance against France.

It is therefore clear that much work remains to be done on Anglo-Russian relations in this period. In particular findings from other series in the Public Record Office, and from other archives, need to be integrated with the already well-known State Papers, Russia, series. It is only when this is done that a more complete picture will emerge of the development of Anglo-Russian relations.

Notes

Unless otherwise stated, all dates are in new style and the year is taken as starting on 1 January.

1.   Bibliothèque Nationale, Nouvelles acquisitions françaises 6834 fol. 55, Villeneuve to the Marquis de Caumont, 28 July 1735.

2. *Sbornik imperatorskago Russkago istoricheskago obshchestvo* (*SIRIO*), 66, p. 444, Lord Harrington, Secretary of State for the Northern Department, to Rondeau, 7 April 1732.

3. Public Record Office, State Papers (PRO, SP) 80/87, Robinson to Harrington, 23 April 1732; *SIRIO*, 66, p. 575, Rondeau to Harrington, 7 April 1733; Dresden, Sachsisches Hauptstaatsarchiv, Geheimes Kabinett, Gesandschaften, 638, IIa fol. 341, De Löss to Augustus III of Saxony-Poland, 23 April 1734; PRO, SP 107/16, Saxon Envoy in London, Bunau, to General DeBrosse, Saxon Envoy Extraordinary at The Hague, 8 September 1733.

4. *SIRIO* 100, Amelot, French Foreign Minister, to Chetardie, French Envoy at St Petersburg, 21 January 1742; Buckinghamshire County Record Office, Trevor Papers, correspondence of Robert Trevor, vols 15, 18, Horatio Walpole to Robert Trevor, Secretary of Embassy at The Hague, 18 November (OS) 1738, 1 May 1739.

5. The Grosse Korrespondenz in Vienna, vol. 97 (b), also contains some Eugene–Liria correspondence.

6. For these *Memoirs* see J. Black, 'Richard Rolt, "Patriot" Historian', *Factotum*, 16 (1983), 19–23.

7. British Library, Additional Manuscripts (BL, Add. MSS) 32686 fols 137, 139, Craggs to Newcastle, 10, 16 August (OS) 1719. Norris and Byng were naval commanders in the Baltic and Mediterranean respectively.

8. BL, Add. MS 32686 fols 320–1, 286–7, Walpole to Newcastle, 31 August (OS), Newcastle to Walpole, 26 July (OS) 1723.

9. BL, Add. MS 32742 fol. 256, Horatio Walpole to Newcastle, 9 March 1725.

10. BL, Add. MS 32750 fol. 413, Newcastle to Horatio Walpole, 28 May (OS) 1727.

11. BL, Add. MSS 32751 fols 220, 284; 32752 fols 167–8, Walpole to Newcastle, 19 August, Townshend, Secretary of State for the Northern Department, to Walpole, 14 August (OS), Walpole to Newcastle, 17 October (OS) 1727.

12. BL, Add. MSS 32768 fols 190–1; 32769 fol. 339, Newcastle to Horatio Walpole, Poyntz and Waldegrave, 2 July (OS), Newcastle to Waldegrave, 28 September (OS) 1730.

13. BL, Add. MSS 32753 fol. 37; 32799 fols 339–40, Keene to

Newcastle, 24 November 1727, Waldegrave to Newcastle, 25 December 1727.

14. BL, Add. MS 38507 fol. 234, Townshend to George II, no date.

15. BL, Add. MSS 37391 fols 49–50; 37392 fols 75–6, 153, Whitworth to Schaub, 24 February, Whitworth to Tilson, 23 August, 4 November 1723.

16. For example, on Peter I's support for the Jacobites in 1724. PRO, SP, 35/50, fols 20–23, Anon. to Anon., no date but endorsed 8 June (OS) 1724.

17. PRO, SP 36/53 fol. 84, Walpole to . . . , 17 October (OS) 1740.

18. *SIRIO* 76, pp. 24, 45, Forbes to Harrington, 6, 28 July (OS) 1733; BL, Add. MS 23789 fol. 36, Forbes to Robinson, 2 August (OS) 1733; PRO, SP 107/16, Count Philip Kinsky, Austrian Envoy Extraordinary in London, to the Emperor Charles VI, 11 September 1733.

19. PRO, SP 107/15, 107/16, Sparre to the Swedish minister Count Horn, 21, 25 August, 11 September 1733. The translation used is that of the British decipherer and translator. PRO, SO 107/5 contains evidence of an interesting discussion between Harrington and the Danish Envoy Count Rantzau, on the Russian naval threat in the Baltic, Rantzau to Count Rosenkrantz, 25 March 1732.

20. PRO, SP 78/189 fol. 260, 75/59 fol. 68, Newcastle to Horatio Walpole, 20 June (OS) 1728, Harrington to Titley, 11 February (OS) 1732; PRO, SP 80/99, Robinson to Harrington, 9 September 1733, on the British wish not to anger Sweden; BL, Add. MS 32782 fol. 244, Waldegrave to Newcastle, 2 October 1733, on Swedish fears.

21. PRO, SP 84/294 fols 134, 138, [Horatio Walpole], Considerations . . . , no date but July–August 1727.

22. PRO, SP 84/316 fols 74–5, Chesterfield to Harrington, 11 January 1732.

23. PRO, SP 80/85, Robinson to Harrington, 11 February 1732; PRO, SP 80/99, 80/100, Robinson to Harrington, 9, 18 September, 28 October; Harrington to Robinson, 18 September (OS), 2 October (OS), Papier rémis par le Comte de Sinzendorf à Mr Robinson, 18 September 1733.

24. PRO, SP 80/84, Robinson to Harrington, 12 January 1732; BL, Add. MS 32778 fol. 245, Robinson to Newcastle, 30 September 1732.

25. The British were also bitterly opposed to the Brunswick–Bevern–Russian marriage scheme, PRO, SP 80/86, Harrington to Robinson, 17 March (OS) 1732.
26. PRO, SP 80/78, 80/84, Harrington to Robinson, 27 August (OS) 1731, 11 January (OS) 1732.
27. PRO, SP 80/84, Robinson to Harrington, 5 January 1732.
28. PRO, SP 80/100, Robinson to Edward Weston, Under-Secretary of State at the Northern Department, 31 October 1733; PRO, SP 90/35, 90/36, Guy Dickens, Secretary at Berlin, to Harrington, 5 December 1733, 20 February 1734; PRO, SP 80/100, Robinson to Harrington, 22 October, 5 December 1733.
29. PRO, SP 80/98, 80/100, 80/101, 80/117, Robinson to Harrington, 24 August, 14 October, 11 November 1733, 5 August 1735; PRO, SP 90/40, Dickens to Tilson, 2 July 1735. In January 1731, a drunken Frederick William I declared 'He would beat them, the English, and the whole world were the Muscovites his friends', PRO, SP 90/30, Dickens to Harrington, 16 January 1731. Whitworth predicted that if Peter I kept Livonia, 'he would perpetually hang over Prussia, like a storm ready to break, and thereby oblige them almost blindly to follow, the dictates of his will', PRO, SP 90/14, Whitworth to Townshend, 12 April 1721.
30. PRO, SP 80/133, enclosed in Robinson to Weston, 25 February 1739.
31. PRO, SP 90/15, 90/19, Whitworth to Tilson, 1 July 1720; Townshend to Du Bourgay, 29, 31 October 1725.
32. PRO, SP 82/42 fols 91, 98, Wych to Tilson, 23 March, Wych to Townshend, 30 March 1725; Norfolk Records Office, Bradfer-Lawrence Collection, Townshend State Papers and Letters, Horatio Walpole to Townshend, 30 May 1728; PRO, SP 82/63, fol. 167; 82/56, fol. 163, Wych to Harrington, 23 December 1741, Harrington to Wych, 19 December (OS) 1735.
33. PRO, SP 82/42 fol. 90, Wych to Tilson, 23 March 1725.
34. PRO, SP 88/29, Edward Finch to Townshend, 24 March 1725.
35. PRO, SP 88/29, 88/30, Townshend to Finch, 30 March (OS), 14 September, 11, 19 October, Finch to Townshend, 21 March, 4 April, 3, 20, 31 October 1725.

British Residents and Visitors in Russia During the Reign of Catherine the Great: Tapped and Untapped Sources from British Archives

ANTHONY G. CROSS

Ten years ago I published an article entitled 'The British in Catherine's Russia: A Preliminary Survey'.[1] Although it was based on a wide range of material gathered over the preceding five years, the word 'preliminary' was used, as it has turned out, advisedly. The ensuing years have clearly shown that the iceberg, the tip of which had been described with some confidence, was itself of far greater proportions than had been imagined. It was, however, to be expected that further research could not but produce a significant yield of new printed and archival sources, illuminating the activities of the British during the long reign of Catherine. If I now venture forth with a survey of materials in British archives, both public and private, I do so with the awareness that the investigation which is currently being carried out by Janet Hartley may well show it to be far from comprehensive.

It is not, however, with archival holdings that I intend to begin, but with published materials, for it is only within the context of what has been published that the significance of what remains can properly be assessed. The published sources may be said to fall into two major categories—those published during the author's own lifetime or prepared by him for publication, and those published posthumously, essentially archival materials, selected and arranged by an editor.

British interest in Russia during Catherine's reign reached unprecedented heights and brought a veritable flood of publications of all kinds. One manifestation of that interest was the first publication of important original British accounts of Russia relating to the first decades of the eighteenth century—such were John Bell's *Travels* (1764), John Cook's *Voyages and Travels* (1770), Jane Rondeau's *Letters* (1775) and Peter Henry Bruce's *Memoirs* (1782); another was the translation of numerous foreign works relating both to the earlier and the contemporary periods—such as those by Algarotti (1769), Manstein (1770), Chappe d'Auteroche (1770), Lesseps (1790) and Chantreau (1794). But it is the works emanating from British residents and travellers in Catherine's Russia and published at that time or shortly afterwards that are of immediate concern. Twenty authors, representing virtually the complete range of 'types', were responsible for some twenty-five publications, equally illustrative of most of the genres to which works on Russia might be allotted. First into the lists was the British Ambassador in 1765–7, Sir George Macartney (1737–1806), with his *Account of Russia* (1768), a self-styled 'Russian almanack for the year 1767'.[2] An appendix to the volume was an essay on the Russian church by the Revd John Glen King (1732–87), who was Chaplain to the British Factory in St Petersburg from 1763 to 1774. King was soon to publish an impressive opus on the *Rites and Ceremonies of the Greek Church, in Russia* (1772) and an essay on the Russian climate (1778).[3] His successor as chaplain was the Revd William Tooke (1774–1820), one of the most prolific authors on Russia, who produced a steady stream of biographies, histories and translations, culminating in a formidable three-volume *View of the Russian Empire* (1799).[4] Tooke, who preferred artful compilation to original composition, contributed, however, thirteen letters to the *Gentleman's Magazine* in 1785–7, describing a journey he made through the Ukraine to the Sea of Azov. Tooke hid his indentity under the initials M.M.M. (the family motto: *Militia mea multiplex*); it was under the pseudonym 'Arcticus' that another prominent member of the British community in St Petersburg sent his numerous and varied articles on Russia to the Edinburgh journal *The Bee* in the 1790s.[5] Matthew Guthrie (1743–1807), a FRS like King and Tooke, was one of the many British doctors in Russian service (from 1769 until his death in 1807), whose scholarly and scientific interests went far beyond medicine.

Three further publications came from British residents, who exemplify other characteristic types—the merchant, the skilled specialist in Russian service (in this case an engraver) and the tutor. In 1762 a description of the recent revolution in Russia and of the death of Peter III was published in the form of a letter from Paul Gilchrist, a merchant of the British Factory.[6] If such a publication were designed to satisfy contemporary British interest in a highly topical event, the work by James Walker (1760?–1822?), Catherine's Court engraver from 1784 to 1796, appeared only in 1821, when many of the personalities it describes were long since dead.[7] Published anonymously, *Paramythia* has been completely overlooked by scholars but is an important source for the social mores of St Petersburg high society and the British community. Idiosyncratic in form, a series of introductions to individual anecdotes or 'scraps', to use Walker's term, *Paramythia* represents the rich genre of anecdotal literature that emerged in the eighteenth and nineteenth centuries and to which, to judge by its title, the third work would also seem to belong. But *Anecdotes of the Russian Empire* (1784) is in almost every way a typical tourist account, couched in the much favoured form of letters to a real or imaginary correspondent. The way in which *Anecdotes* differs, apart from the fact that it is better written than most, is that its author, William Richardson (1743–1814), was strictly speaking not a tourist but a resident, employed during the period 1768–72 as tutor to the sons of Lord Cathcart, the British Ambassador.[8]

It was Catherine's reign, however, that saw the emergence of the 'Northern Tour', a variant on the usual itinerary of the 'Grand Tour', and many British tourists made their way to the Russian capital. It was from their ranks that there came a comparatively small number of authentic accounts, supplemented by several compilations from armchair travellers. If Henry Nebel in his travel bibliography blithely accepts as genuine the works by William Thomson and John Richard (as well as that by Chantreau),[9] contemporaries were much more on their guard. Of Richard's *Tour from London to Petersburgh* (1780), Jeremy Bentham wrote, 'no such person I dare swear—a catch-penny performance—an imposture'[10] (and indeed nothing has ever been established about the author of this superficial and

imprecise work), the *Annual Register* was sceptical about Joseph
Marshall's *Travels* (1772) and, somewhat later, another writer
noted that 'Marshall has published travels through various
parts of Europe without once having crossed the Channel'.[11]
Similar doubts were voiced about Lady Craven's *Journey through
the Crimea* (1789) and Andrew Swinton's *Travels into Norway,
Denmark and Russia* (1792),[12] but both authors travelled when
and where they stated, which could not be said about William
Thomson (1746–1821), the author of the anonymously published *Letters from Scandinavia* (1796), who plundered the
wrongly maligned Swinton as well as a string of other accounts
including, notably, the justly famed *Travels into Poland, Russia,
Sweden, and Denmark* by William Coxe.[13]

Coxe (1747–1828), who had gone to Russia for the first time
in 1778–9 as tutor or 'bear-leader' to the young Lord Herbert
(1759–1827), reveals all the strengths and weaknesses of the
donnish traveller, who later reworks his material in the quiet of
his study, adding to his diary of things seen and done a vast
amount of historical, literary and geographical information
gleaned from the best authorities. The first edition appeared in
1784 and was followed by two further editions in 1785 and
1787, before the first edition was itself completed in 1790 by a
third supplementary volume, which included material from
Coxe's second Russian visit in 1784–5, when he was tutor to
Samuel Whitbread II (1764–1815). Three further rearranged
and expanded versions were to appear by 1802. Coxe became
more or less the Baedeker of the eighteenth century; people
would take his bulky volumes on their own travels; travellers
would test their own impressions against his; mothers, indeed,
would follow from afar their sons' progress by reference to his
work.

Coxe, Lady Craven (1750–1828), Swinton, Nathaniel Wraxall
(1751–1831), author of an aptly entitled *Cursory Remarks Made in
a Tour through some of the Northern Parts of Europe*(1775), and
Thomas Randolph, now credited with *Observations on the Present
State of Denmark, Russia, and Switzerland* (1784), make up the
small group of publishing tourists during the reign of Catherine
II; to their number may be added the further names of Sir John
Sinclair (1754–1835), who made use of a parliamentary recess to
make a lightning trip to St Petersburg in 1786–7 and soon after

his return published privately for friends and political figures
his assessment of Russia under the title of *General Observations
Regarding the Present State of the Russian Empire* (1787),[14] and of
George Forster, an employee of the East India Company returning from India to England on a long journey that took him from
Astrakhan to Moscow and St Petersburg in 1784 and of which he
published much later a generally worthless (as regards its few
pages on Russia) description.[15] Finally, records of Russian experiences of a somewhat different kind are to be found in the
writings of the smallpox inoculator Dr Thomas Dimsdale (1712–
1800) and of the prison reformer and philanthropist John
Howard (1726–90). Dimsdale included a description of his
visit to Russia in 1768–9 and of his successful inoculation of
Catherine and her son, the Grand Duke Paul, as the first of his
Tracts on Inoculation (1781), and John Howard, who was to die in
the south of Russia on a second visit in 1790, incorporated
impressions of Russian prison conditions from his first visit in
1781 in the third edition (1784) of his celebrated *State of the
Prisons*.

It was early in the nineteenth century that we encounter the
first instance of the posthumous publication of materials relating
to Russia. In 1812 there appeared the anonymous *Letters from the
Continent: Describing the Manners and Customs of Germany, Poland,
Russia, and Switzerland, in the Years 1790, 1791, and 1792; to a
Friend Residing in England*. The unknown editor, who would
seem to have been the recipient of the letters, speaks of the
author as 'an elegant classical scholar, and an accomplished
gentleman', who had died some years previously and whom
recent scholarship has identified as Lionel Colmore (1765–
1807).[16] The letters are those of a typical tourist, whose un-
guarded and scathing comments on Russian society were des-
tined for the eyes of an intimate friend and not for publication,
but which fell victim to Russian *perelyustratsiya*, as the absence of
certain of the St Petersburg letters suggests. *Letters from the
Continent* was, however, not typical of subsequent archival publications in the nineteenth and early twentieth centuries; the
emphasis was moved on to the man rather than on to the country.
It was in the biographies and collected writings and correspondence of men eminent in diplomacy, politics, learning or
society who at some stage of their careers resided in Russia that

interesting new material is to be found. Not surprisingly, former ambassadors to the Court of Catherine figure prominently, with particularly extensive selections from the correspondence and dispatches of John, 2nd Earl of Buckinghamshire (1729–93), in 1900–2 and of Sir James Harris (1746–1820) in 1845.[17] Inevitable accounts of the life and good works of John Howard appeared (1818 and 1855) in which new Russian materials were introduced;[18] and without any attempt at an exhaustive listing, one might mention the biographies of Samuel Bentham (1862), Mary Kinnersley, Baroness de Bode (1900), Sir Gilbert Elliot (1874), Sir George Macartney (1906), Lord Granville Leveson-Gower (1916) and Charlotte, Countess Bentinck (1912) as works containing often unexpected archival material, principally letters, from British residents and visitors.[19]

The seeking out and publication of archival sources, of which the interest lies primarily in what is being described rather than in the author, is essentially a modern phenomenon, and with respect to Catherine's Russia and other early periods of Russian history, a consequence of the growth of academic Russian studies. Scholarly journals within the last twenty years have carried a small number of articles relevant to our theme with documents drawn from private and public collections and illustrating aspects of the life of the British community in St Petersburg.[20] It was as a condensed version of a very bulky manuscript in private hands that the only new addition to the literature of the Northern Tour appeared in 1971, as part of what was otherwise a reprint series of early foreign accounts of Russia. The travel diaries of the Oxford don John Parkinson (1754–1840) proved an exciting and significant discovery on several counts. Parkinson, unlike Coxe, was not constrained by thoughts of publication, and the diaries keep intact a wealth of gossip, anecdotes, personal detail, and random jottings on every conceivable topic that are of value for the historian of Catherine's time (and indeed of the British community). He was writing at a particularly interesting period (1792–4), which is scarcely reflected in earlier published British accounts; his itinerary took him well beyond the usual tourist route—to Siberia as far as Tobol'sk, then south to the Caspian and the foothills of the Caucasus, across to the Crimea, and then back north through the Ukraine to Moscow and St Petersburg.[21] Two more recent publications

have contributed importantly to our knowledge of British activities in Russia in the immediately preceding period of Catherine's
reign. In 1959 the Navy Records Society published *A Memoir of
James Trevenen*, edited from a manuscript originally prepared
by his brother-in-law Admiral Sir Charles Penrose in 1805.
Trevenen died in 1790 in the Russian action against the Swedes
off Vyborg, and his letters are a unique source of information
on the often fraught relations between the British officers in
Russian service and their Russian counterparts. In the Russian
navy during the earlier campaign against the Turks (1787–8)
was Samuel Bentham (1757–1831) and it is the monumental
edition of the collected works of his brother Jeremy (1748–1832)
being issued by the Athlone Press that illuminates their strong
Russian connection which began before Samuel departed for
Russia in 1780 and continued after his return in 1791. Volumes
2–4 of Jeremy's correspondence cover the main Russian years
and present for the first time the diary and related letters of
Jeremy during his own visit to see his brother at Krichev in the
Ukraine in 1786–7, as well as substantial portions of Samuel's
vastly informative and entertaining letters from Russia for the
period 1780–91.

The Bentham edition highlights in dramatic fashion the
riches that still remain in British archives for the study of
Catherine's Russia; at the same time, since the emphasis is on
Jeremy rather than on Samuel and other correspondents, future
researchers may well need to consult the manuscripts for
material not considered relevant for the purposes of the edition.
It is only to be expected that the jottings in a notebook, documents from extraneous sources, bills and other ephemera which
may contain precious details for a scholar are not of themselves
worthy of publication, but there may of course be more substantial items, the diary of Samuel Bentham's journey to Siberia in
1781–2 among the Bentham Papers in the British Library being
a case in point.[22] I shall therefore include in my survey of
archival sources collections associated with some of the authors
already mentioned, principally of the self-publishing kind.

Ambassadors are traditionally great hoarders, and if their
official dispatches are held in the Public Record Office, copies,
together with their extensive correspondence and other papers,
are found in their private collections, which may or may not

have made their way to public repositories. The Earl of Bucking-hamshire's papers are now in the Norfolk Record Office, for instance, part of Macartney's are in the Public Record Office of Northern Ireland in Belfast, some of Harris's papers are at Merton College, Oxford, and others remain in the family, and were used by Isabel de Madariaga in her book on the Armed Neutrality.[23] In addition to the Buckinghamshire and Macartney papers, I have had the opportunity to see the papers of three more ambassadors to Catherine's court, Lord Charles Cathcart, Alleyne Fitzherbert (later Lord St Helens), and Sir Charles Whitworth (later Baron Whitworth). Whitworth (1752–1825) was in Russia from 1788 to 1800, but his papers among the Sackville of Knole Manuscripts in the Kent Archives Office at Maidstone refer virtually exclusively to the reign of Paul, although documents relating to his dealings with members of the British Factory in St Petersburg and Riga are of wider interest.[24] The same is largely true of the Fitzherbert Manu-scripts in the Derbyshire Record Office at Matlock, for Fitz-herbert (1753–1839) had two spells in Russia, 1783–7 and 1801–2. However, although the second embassy is better represented, there are numerous earlier documents of a diplomatic nature, translations of Russian documents, memoranda, miscellaneous correspondence with various members of the British com-munity. It was from a notebook of highly disparate materials by different hands that I learnt, for instance, of the establishment of a branch of the Order of the Beggar's Benison, a notorious Scottish hell-fire club, in St Petersburg in 1773.[25]

Through the invitation and gracious hospitality of the present Lord Cathcart I was able to examine at his home in Cawdor the papers of his ancestor (1721–76), which were of a much more personal nature and, for my own particular researches, proved more informative than the other collections. The main item was the diary in twenty-four little volumes, mainly in French, which Lady Jane Cathcart had kept from 1745 until just before her death in St Petersburg in November 1771; volumes 20–24 covered their life in Russia and reveal the diarist as a deeply religious woman, a devoted mother and wife, and an interested and intelligent observer of the Russian scene. In addition there are two folders of correspondence for the Russian years which contain valuable details about Anglo-Russian relations, particularly cultural.[26] A certain amount of Cathcart correspondence is to be found in the British Library, which also holds the papers of Sir Robert Keith, who served from 1758 through the short reign of Peter III and the first months of Catherine's, and of Sir Robert Gunning, Cathcart's successor.[27]

The British Library not unexpectedly holds a wealth of relevant material. It is there, for instance, that the extensive Coxe Papers are also to be found, containing much of the raw material from which he fashioned the successive editions of his travels and some that he felt it necessary to suppress, as well as interesting correspondence, including a number of long letters from the ubiquitous Matthew Guthrie, whose own substantial archive is also in the British Library.[28] Guthrie, who acted as much more than an editor for *A Tour through the Taurida, or Crimea*, published under his wife's name in 1802, left in manuscript 'A Supplementary Tour through the Countries in the Black Sea Conquered by Russia from the Turks', completed in two volumes in 1805, a translation of Catherine's historical play *Nachal'noe upravlenie Olega*, and the original English version of a work on Russian folklore and customs eventually published in French as *Dissertations sur les antiquités de Russie* (1795).[29]

'... keep a Journal, which will be a great Amusement to us, as well as useful to yourself.'[30] As far as is known, Lord Granville Leveson-Gower, visiting St Petersburg in 1792, did not heed his mother's advice, but many other travellers filled their notebooks with their impressions of peoples and places for the diversion of their families and friends. A surprising number of these journals and diaries survive. Although Parkinson's recently published journals are far and away the most detailed and extensive (there are incidentally also a number of his letters from Russia in the Lincolnshire Records Office),[31] others contain much of interest, and perhaps three of the eight I have examined might well be published with profit for the student of Catherine's Russia. Indeed, I have prepared for publication the journal of Baroness Elizabeth Dimsdale (1732–1812), who accompanied her husband on his second visit to Russia in 1781 to inoculate the Grand Dukes Alexander and Constantine. It is part of the unique Dimsdale family archive, rich in paintings, porcelain and other possessions, connected with the two momentous visits of Thomas Dimsdale, and in letters sent by him from Russia and received from such as Grand Duke Paul and Father Andrei Samborskii, the long-serving Russian priest in London.[32] The journal is gossipy, anecdotal, endlessly revealing about the writer herself and the numerous Russians and British she met; it gives an unrivalled picture of life at Tsarskoe Selo and fascinating glimpses of the Imperial family.

An equally privileged insight into Russian high society fell to the lot of Katherine Harris, who accompanied her brother Sir James and his wife to St Petersburg in the autumn of 1777, returned again at the very beginning of 1783 and remained until the end of Harris's appointment. Both visits are described in her diaries; in 1778 she also spent two months in Moscow, which she records in some detail in a separate notebook.[33] Miss Harris was a devoted theatre-goer, and her descriptions of plays and performances provide information unavailable in any other source, Russian or foreign. Among the Englishmen mentioned in her 1783 journal is Samuel Bentham, recently returned from Siberia; and it was with Bentham at Potemkin's Ukrainian estate of Krichev that the noted antiquarian Sir Richard Worsley (1751– 1805) was to stay for a month in the summer of 1786. Worsley had landed in the Crimea and made his way north to Moscow and St Petersburg, before leaving overland via Poland. Despite an annoying propensity to write simply 'ditto' to indicate his continued stay in one place, he did commit to his diary a record of his doings and meetings; of particular interest are his comments on the Moscow theatrical impresario Michael Maddox and his various enterprises.[34] Yet another English visitor to Russia who was closely connected with the Benthams was Reginald Pole Carew (1753–1835), whose archive remains with the family at Antony House in Cornwall. Carew stayed with Samuel Bentham in St Petersburg at the end of 1780, following his arrival from Scandinavia; after some nine months in the capital, he journeyed home via Moscow and the Crimea. His archive is of great interest and includes, in addition to correspondence with such as Potemkin, much material of various types relating to his travels. While there is no journal as such, there are what amount to chapters for a book on the 'present state of Russia'; it seems that he abandoned the project on learning of Coxe's intention to publish, and it is known from his letters that he supplied Coxe with a good deal of information and read his *Travels* in proof.[35]

It is from 1774, only four years before Coxe's visit, that there dates the earliest of the unpublished accounts that I have found. The Russian section of the journal of John Jervis (1735–1823) (better known by his later title of the Earl of St Vincent) is a mere hundred sides of small format in length and records a month's sojourn in St Petersburg. Predictably, the author manifests a particular interest in naval matters and an occasional vigorous turn of phrase, for instance in his description of 'the Baths, which represented such a monstrous Scene of beastly Women & indecent men mix'd together naked as our first parents without the least appearance of Shame, as to shock our feelings'.[36] Two years later another military man visited the Russian capital for an identical period, did much the same things, and left an even more succinct account. Much more taken with members of the British Factory than with any Russians he met and generally dismissive of what he saw, the author left St Petersburg with no obvious regret. The regret was all mine that the journal, which I examined in February this year, proved not to be the gold-mine I had hoped, for not only had more than twelve years passed since I had first learned of its existence and had been refused permission to see it by its then owner, but its compiler was none other than Patrick Brydone (1736–1818), author of the famous *Tour through Sicily and Malta* (1773 and constantly re-published).[37]

If *libri habent sui fatelli*, so do manuscripts. When Nebel's bibliography of travel accounts appeared, I was intrigued by an entry describing *A Northern Tour in the Years 1775 and 1776*, said to be written by John, 2nd Lord Henniker. The item was marked as unseen, and Professor Nebel in reply to my letter wrote that he could not remember where he had seen the reference. The present Lord Henniker, to whom I then turned for assistance, did not know of the work, but suggested it may have been sold at the sale of the library at Thornham Hall before the Second World War. And it appears that this was in fact the case. For my plea for information in the first number (1973) of the *Newsletter* of the Study Group on Eighteenth-Century Russia brought, totally unexpectedly, three years later, an answer from a member of the Group, Philip Longworth, who had bought the work shortly before from a leading London bookseller, who had acquired it at a sale in South America. The work turned out to be a fascinating manuscript journal, written as a series of letters and illustrated by the author, of travels through Denmark to St Petersburg.[38] A further reminder that similar but hitherto unknown works might surface at any time came very recently, when Sothebys offered the chemist Charles Hatchett's journal of his visit to Russia in 1790–1, along with twenty letters he sent during that time to his father, John, the famous coachbuilder, whose carriages were much sought by the Russian aristocracy.[39]

It is obvious that the diaries and journals which I have listed constitute an important corpus of virtually untapped material on Catherine's Russia. With the exception of Pole Carew, the writers had no publishing pretensions, at least as far as their work on Russia is concerned, and their writings generally lack the considered and polished essays on serfdom, trade, culture, history and similar subjects that distinguish the works of Richardson and Coxe. The emphasis is on the immediate reaction to places and people, the retailing of good anecdote or a bit of court scandal, and the detailing of what seemed significant or worthy of record for themselves or, at most, a correspondent. Their writings are sprinkled with the names of people which would have been meaningless to the contemporary English reading public and with the minutiae in which it would have had little interest. But it is precisely these aspects which are attractive to the historian who is in search of the particular rather than the general, the detail that helps to explain a certain occurrence or give life to a certain person. To a marked degree this is true of the remaining material which I wish to introduce.

If the preceding group of writings emanated from tourists and short-term visitors, there is another corpus of materials, heterogeneous in character and provenance, but essentially connected with members of the British community in St Petersburg. The materials are largely but not exclusively letters, and their writers or recipients belong to the category exemplified only in part by the publishing authors Tooke, Guthrie and Walker. The merchants were the heart of the British community, but it is not surprising that they were among the least likely candidates for literary fame. Yet any documents which might breathe life into the readily available tables of exports and imports, the lists of British merchant houses or the generally dry and factual records of the Russia Company (housed, incidentally, in the Guildhall

Library, London) can only be welcomed. There are among the papers of British ambassadors to Catherine's court letters and petitions from merchants requesting assistance or protection, but there are other small collections of correspondence from merchants to their relations or partners in Britain which are informative about the workings of merchant houses, the forming and dissolving of partnerships, the characters of people involved, relationships with other firms or with the Russian authorities. Walter Shairp was a merchant in St Petersburg from 1748 until his death in 1787 and for the last decade Consul-General to the Factory; a number of letters from him to his father over the period 1748–71 survive among the Shairp of Houston Papers in the Scottish Record Office.[40] It was in 1772 that Robert Duesbury jun. of Scarborough went to the Russian capital and soon set up in partnership with Atkins and Rigail; seven of his letters to his sister, along with various other legal documents and his will, are to be found in the Hull University Library.[41] Among his executors was John Cayley, who himself was to become British Consul-General in 1787, and his own will, unexpectedly coming up for sale at the end of 1984, was acquired by the Brotherton Library of Leeds University. It is also at Leeds that there are now to be found the papers of the Cattleys, yet another of the great Anglo-Russian families living in Russia way beyond the period covered by my survey. Stephen Cattley, the first of the family to go to Russia in 1772, in fact joined the firm of Atkins, Rigail and Duesbury, and when Robert Duesbury returned to England in 1777, Cattley became a partner in his stead. 'A Narrative Private and Commercial', composed by Stephen Cattley, as well as a whole series of letters from his brother-in-law John Cattley, who was in St Petersburg in 1785–6, remain with another branch of the family, but will also be coming to Leeds in the near future.[42]

Perhaps the most revealing source on the less attractive sides of the merchant community is the group of letters sent in the 1790s by the son of Baron Sutherland to Samuel Whitbread (whom he had met in St Petersburg in 1785); these letters, published in substantial extracts by me in an article in the *Slavonic and East European Review*, are in the Bedfordshire Record Office.[43] Letters from merchants are in the set of letters addressed to James Mounsey (1700?–73), the distinguished

Scottish doctor who served under Elizabeth, Peter III and Catherine II before retiring to Scotland and petitioning unsuccessfully for a baronetcy; these letters, recently discovered in the National Library of Wales, cover the period from 1747 to shortly before Mounsey's death in 1773, although the majority date from Catherine's reign.[44] Evidence of the vigorous trade between England and Russia is contained in the Manvers Papers at the University of Nottingham, which deal with the setting up of the Duchess of Kingston's estate near Narva on the Baltic in the early 1780s. Bills for shipments of plants and trees and livestock are found alongside letters from her steward and gardener whom she brought to Russia.[45] Finally, mention might be made of the Hynam Papers deposited in the Greater London Record Office: the bulk of the papers date from the nineteenth century but the earlier ones are informative on the activity of Robert Hynam (1737–1818), watchmaker to the Empress.[46]

It has naturally not been possible or even necessary to list all the archival sources that are available to help build up a much more closely detailed picture of the British in Catherine's Russia than has hitherto been attempted. There exist numerous other documents and letters in numerous private and public archives that are written by or relate to British residents and visitors—Dr Appleby has demonstrated the wealth of such material with regard to British doctors, only two or three of whom have been mentioned. Two final observations might, however, be made: the British archival sources are only one side of what is very much an Anglo-Russian subject, and Soviet archives undoubtedly contain a great deal of material, some of which will never become known or made available to foreign researchers; secondly, it can only be a matter of regret that some of the most outstanding British residents have left no personal records of their activities. One would willingly surrender the travel journals of almost any of the tourists for the diaries of such as the architect Charles Cameron (1746?–1812), the doctor John Rogerson (1741–1823), the admiral Samuel Greig (1735–88), or the gardener John Bush (1730?–95), all holding high positions in imperial service. But such sources seem not to exist, certainly not in Great Britain, and we must remain thankful for the significant holdings we possess.

Notes

1. In *The Eighteenth Century in Russia*, edited by J. G. Garrard (Oxford, 1973), pp. 233–63.

2. On Macartney, see Michael Roberts, *Macartney in Russia, The English Historical Review*, Supplement 7 (London, 1974).

3. *Letter to the Right Reverend the Lord Bishop of Durham Containing some Observations on the Climate of Russia, and the Northern Countries* (London, 1778). On King, see my 'Chaplains to the British Factory in St Petersburg, 1723–1813', *European Studies Review*, 2, no. 2 (1972), 132–3.

4. See my 'The Reverend William Tooke's Contribution to English Knowledge of Russia at the End of the Eighteenth Century', *Canadian Slavic Studies*, 3, no. 1 (1969), 106–15.

5. See my 'Arcticus and *The Bee*', *Oxford Slavonic Papers* (*OSP*), New Series 2 (1969), 62–76. See also K. A. Papmehl, 'Matthew Guthrie—the Forgotten Student of Eighteenth-Century Russia', *Canadian Slavonic Papers*, 11, no. 2 (1969), 167–81.

6. *A Genuine Letter to Mr Saunders, Giving a Particular and Circumstantial Account of the Great Revolution in Russia and the Death of Peter III* (London, 1762).

7. See my 'James Walker's *Paramythia*', *Study Group on Eighteenth-Century Russia Newsletter*, 3 (1975), 41–51.

8. See H. Pitcher, 'A Scottish View of Catherine's Russia: William Richardson's *Anecdotes of the Russian Empire* (1784)', *Forum for Modern Language Studies*, 3, no. 3 (1967), 236–51.

9. H. Nebel, *To Russia and Return* (Columbus, Ohio, 1968), nos 102, 120, 125.

10. *The Correspondence of Jeremy Bentham*, edited by Timothy L. S. Sprigge (London, 1968), II, 124.

11. *Annual Register for 1772* (1773), p. 241; John Parkinson, *A Tour of Russia, Siberia and the Crimea 1792–1794*, edited by William Collier (London, 1971), p. 11.

12. *Gentleman's Magazine*, 59 (1789), 287–8; *Critical Review*, New Series 5 (1792), 294–9.

13. The *Dictionary of National Biography*, LVI (1898), 275, does not mention *Letters from Scandinavia*, but credits Thomson with the authorship of Swinton's *Travels*.

14. See my '"Zamechaniia" Sera Dzhona Sinklera o Rossii', in *XVIII vek*, 10 (Leningrad, 1975), 160–8.

15. *A Journey from Bengal to England, through the Northern Part of India, Kashmire, Afghanistan, and Persia, and into Russia, by the Caspian Sea*, 2 vols (London, 1796).

16. Gavin de Beer, 'An Anonymous Identified: Lionel Colmore (1765–1807)', *Notes and Queries* (August 1967), 303–4.

17. *The Despatches and Correspondence of John, Second Earl of Buckinghamshire, Ambassador to the Court of Catherine II of Russia 1762–1765*, edited by Adelaide D'Arcy Collyer, 2 vols (London, 1900–2); *Diaries and Correspondence of James Harris, First Earl of Malmesbury*, edited by his grandson, the third Earl, 2 vols (London, 1844).

18. James Baldwin Brown, *Memoirs of the Public and Private Life of John Howard, the Philanthropist* (London, 1818); J. Field, *Correspondence of John Howard, the Philanthropist, not Before Published* (London, 1855).

19. M. S. Bentham, *The Life of Brigadier-General Sir Samuel Bentham, KSG* (London, 1862); William S. Childe-Pemberton, *The Baroness de Bode 1775–1803* (London, 1900); *Life and Letters of Sir Gilbert Elliot, First Earl of Minto*, edited by his great niece the Countess of Minto, I (London, 1874); Helen H. Robbins, *Our First Ambassador to China: An Account of the Life of George, Earl of Macartney* (London, 1908); *Lord Granville Leveson Gower: Private Correspondence 1781 to 1821*, edited by his daughter-in-law Castalia, Countess Granville, 2 vols (London, 1916); Mrs Aubrey Le Blond, *Charlotte Sophie Countess Bentinck: Her Life and Times, 1715–1800*, 2 vols (London, 1912).

20. See James Cracaft, 'James Brogden in Russia, 1787–1788', *Slavonic and East European Review (SEER)*, 47 (1969), 219–44; A. G. Cross, 'British Freemasons in Russia during the Reign of Catherine the Great', *OSP*, New Series 4 (1971), 43–72.

21. See my 'An Oxford Don in Catherine the Great's Russia', *Journal of European Studies*, 1, no. 2 (1971), 166–74.

22. British Library (BL), Add. MS 33552, fols 110–292. Considerable use has been made of Samuel Bentham's papers by scholars in recent years: Matthew S. Anderson, 'Samuel

Bentham in Russia, 1779–1791', *Slavic Review (SR)*, 15, no. 2 (1956), 157–72; Walther Kirchner, 'Samuel Bentham and Siberia', *SEER*, 36 (1958), 471–80; K. A. Papmehl, 'The Regimental School Established in Siberia by Samuel Bentham', *Canadian Slavonic Papers*, 8 (1966), 153–68; K. A. Papmehl, 'Samuel Bentham and the *Sobesednik*', *SEER*, 46 (1968), 210–19; I. R. Christie, 'Samuel Bentham and the Western Colony at Krichev, 1784–1787', *SEER*, 48 (1970), 232–47; I. R. Christie, 'Samuel Bentham and the Russian Dnieper Flotilla 1787–1788', *SEER*, 50 (1972), 173–97.

23.   Norfolk Record Office, Buckinghamshire Papers, NRS 21120–2, 21408–10, etc; Public Record Office of Northern Ireland, Macartney Papers, D572; I. M. de Madariaga, *Britain, Russia and the Armed Neutrality of 1780* (London, 1963).

24.   Kent Archives Office, Sackville of Knowle MSS, U 269, 0195–8. See James J. Kenney, jun., 'Lord Whitworth and the Conspiracy against Tsar Paul I: The New Evidence of the Kent Archive', *SR*, 36, no. 2 (1977), 205–19.

25.   Derbyshire Record Office, Fitzherbert Papers, MS 239 m, 0423–755, 0854–79. A. G. Cross, 'The Order of the Beggar's Benison in Russia: An Unknown Episode in Scoto–Russian Relations in the Eighteenth Century', *Scottish Slavonic Review*, 3 (1984), 45–63, based on MS 0478.

26.   Auchindoune, Cawdor, Cathcart Papers, journal of Lady Jane Cathcart and folders H and I.

27.   BL, Add. MSS 35484–95, Keith Papers; Egerton MSS 2696–2706, Gunning Papers; Add. MS 6826, Cathcart Papers.

28.   BL, Add. MSS 9254–7.

29.   BL, Add. MSS 14388–90.

30.   *Lord Granville Leveson Gower*, I, 58.

31.   Lincolnshire Record Office, Dixon MSS 16/6/14–31.

32.   Barkway House, Barkway, Dimsdale Collection. A description of the manuscripts is available at the Hertfordshire Record Office.

33.   Public Record Office, Lowry Cole Papers, 30/43.10–13 and 18–20.

34. Lincolnshire Record Office, Worsley MSS no. 24.
35. Antony House, Torpoint, Carew–Pole MSS, CC/J/11–13, CO/R/3–6. Documents may be consulted by arrangement at the Cornwall Record Office, Truro.
36. BL, Add. MSS 31192.
37. Scottish Record Office (SRO), Adam of Blair Adam MSS 1454/4/438, Journal no. 18. On Brydone, see Paul Fussell, jun., 'Patrick Brydone: The Eighteenth-Century Traveler as Representative Man', *Bulletin of the New York Public Library* (June 1962), 349–63. Fussel was unaware of the material in the Adam of Blair Adam papers, which include no less than twenty-one travel journals as well as military journals and numerous other notebooks for the period 1760–1800, and which would possibly allow a life of this inveterate but little-known traveller at last to be written.
38. 'A Northern Tour in the Years 1775 and 1776 through Copenhagen and Petersburg to the River Swir, Joining the Lakes of Onega and Ladoga in a Series of Letters', MS diary in the possession of Professor Philip Longworth.
39. Sotheby's sale catalogue of 16/17 July 1984, item 396. Other Hatchett documents, including letters from Russian correspondents, are held in the Library of the University College of Wales, Swansea.
40. SRO, Shairp of Houston Papers, GD 30.
41. Brynmor Jones Library, University of Hull, Duesbery Papers, DDDU/20–3.
42. None of the Cattley material at Leeds is as yet sorted or catalogued. I am extremely grateful to Mr Eric Cattley of Kingston, Devon, for supplying me with copies of Stephen Cattley's 'Narrative' and John Cattley's letters.
43. Bedfordshire Record Office, Whitbread Papers, MSS 5699, 4474–81. See my 'The Sutherland Affair and its Aftermath', *SEER*, 50 (1972), 257–75.
44. The thirty-three letters to Mounsey were made known to me by Mr Graham Thomas, Assistant Archivist in the Department of Manuscripts of the University of Wales, who is preparing them for publication.
45. University of Nottingham Library, Manvers Papers, MS 41478.
46. Greater London Record Office, MSS F/PE7/141–75.

A Survey of Some Anglo-Russian Medical and Natural History Material in British Archives, from the Seventeenth Century to the Beginning of the Nineteenth Century

JOHN H. APPLEBY

The aim of this paper is to show that the study of Anglo-Russian medical and natural history is justified in its own right, even on the basis of archival material as opposed to published sources. Although the territory is relatively unexplored, sufficient has been written to provide a reasonable introduction to the subject. Nor is specialized knowledge necessary—anyone with a general interest in medicine and natural history will find that the available material is surprisingly approachable and easy to understand.[1]

For practical purposes I have arranged the survey in chronological order, but with progressions or regressions where groupings under archives or subject matter warrant it. For greater cohesion the material has been structured around key figures who played a crucial part in the development of the theme. Most, but not all of them, were Scottish doctors and surgeons who served in Russia, from where they channelled information to Britain.[2]

British doctors and apothecaries first went to Russia in 1557 as a result of the establishment of diplomatic relations during Ivan the Terrible's reign and the expanded activities of the Russia Company. Many of the doctors were associated with the Royal College of Physicians of London. Some information about them and later doctors may be gleaned from the *Annals of the College of Physicians* (which is also on microfiche), as well as from publications such as Munk's *Roll*.[3] A surviving draft bill of proceedings by the College in the Star Chamber against members of the Society of Apothecaries during 1634 and 1635 reveals that the Apothecaries supplied Russia with medicines in the 1630s on an extensive scale. Arthur, son of the famous John Dee, who had been physician to Tsar Michael for fourteen years before taking up the post of Physician Extraordinary to Charles I, himself testified about these medicines.[4] Unfortunately, search among other records of the Society of Apothecaries at the Guildhall Library, with one or two exceptions, has uncovered little about the export of apothecaries' wares to Russia through the centuries. To some extent this is compensated for by the Court Minute Books of the Russia Company (dating from the Great Fire of London in 1666) and the earliest register of the British Factory's Chapel in Russia, ranging from 1706 to 1815. These, which are also among the archives at the Guildhall Library, often provide brief but useful details of the lives of British doctors and botanists in Russia.[5]

Moving on to the reign of Tsar Alexis, we find a very important event taking place when Samuel Collins, who had been his physician for three years, obtained leave of absence to return to England in 1662. On his arrival he offered to correspond from Russia with the Royal Society of London which had officially been incorporated that same year. The task of formulating questions on Russia devolved largely upon Robert Boyle. In his paper about Boyle's works and Collins's book *The Present State of Russia*, the writer, Leo Loewenson, expertly illustrated Collins's contributions to Boyle's writings, overlooking, however, published and unpublished letters from Collins to Boyle which between them shed even more light on various aspects of Russian medicine and natural history.[6] Samuel Collins wrote two comprehensive tracts while in Russia, one on obesity and the other about the medical uses of the valerian and burdock plants. They and much other valuable material linked with British doctors' contributions to Russian medicine are to be found in Novombergskii's indispensable and very rare work, *Materialy po istorii meditsiny v Rossii*. The five volumes and a supplement can be consulted at the Library of the Wellcome Institute for the History of Medicine.[7]

The Archives of the USSR Academy of Sciences at Leningrad hold the voluminous correspondence belonging to the

Scot Robert Erskine, Peter the Great's chief physician and 'archiater', who directed the entire Russian medical hierarchy and died in 1718. Transcripts of forty letters to Erskine from nineteen English and Scottish correspondents, including Dr Archibald Pitcairne, together with photocopies and a microfilm of letters to Erskine from outstanding figures such as Prince Menshikov and Albert Seba the Dutch apothecary, are available at the Royal Society's Library. Also located there and in the Wellcome Library are transcripts or microfilms of Erskine's diary of Peter's treatment at Carlsbad and his and Pitcairne's library catalogues—both their libraries, regarded as some of the finest of their day, formed the cornerstone of the future academy's library. In addition, transcripts of the medical and natural history sections of the so-called 'Kamerny' catalogue—the first to be published of the Academy's library holdings, have been presented, respectively, to the libraries of the Wellcome Institute and the British Museum (Natural History).[8]

As far as the Royal Society is concerned, a second phase of its interest in Russian medicine and natural history was marked by the setting up of a Committee for Russia on 19 February 1713, with Isaac Newton, Edmund Halley, James Petiver, Richard Mead and John Arbuthnot among its sixteen members. Sloane, Woodward and Halley elaborated on the queries drawn up by the committee and discussed a week later. On 12 March the Russia Committee met again to hear the replies of Charles Whitworth, English resident in Russia, to some of the questions. Letters were read out addressed to Robert Erskine and Henry Farquharson, inviting them to correspond with the Royal Society and enclosing the 'Queries to be answered' as well as copies of Petiver's *Instructions for Collecting Specimens of Plants, Insects and Animals*. The fifty-three 'Enquireys for Russia', wide ranging but concisely formulated, are useful pointers to what interested the British in Russia at the time. Supposing the letters were in fact sent, no replies have been traced, but at least it had been a useful exercise in focusing members' attention on Russian natural history and medicine.[9]

At this point it is worth emphasizing that there are two classics which provide a wealth of factual information about British doctors' activities in Russia. They are Lipskii's bicentenary account of the St Petersburg Botanical Garden—a copy is in the

Botany Department's Library of the Natural History Museum—
and Professor Chistovich's history of the first medical schools in
Russia.[10]

It was during Erskine's influential period of office that
Scottish physicians and surgeons began to arrive in Russia
with recommendations to the 'archiater'. In the course of the
next century Scots doctors, often intermarrying, predominated
over English ones. One of them was John Bell of Antermony
whose book of *Travels* to China and Persia for the Russians is
well known.[11] The papers of Thomas Gordon, Admiral of the
Russian Fleet, at the Scottish Record Office contain a considerable amount about Bell and other Scots in the Russian
service. Although the papers are catalogued in the tenth report
of the Historical Manuscripts Commission, by no means all the
Russian connections are covered, so that an examination of
the originals is essential. The papers and letter books highlight
some of the commercial and professional engagements not only
of Bell, but also of the surgeons William Horn and Francis
Hay.[12]

The Swiss-born Johann Amman made a great contribution to
Anglo-Russian natural history which has largely been overlooked by scholars. Elected a fellow of the Royal Society in 1731,
Amman acted as assistant to the President, Sir Hans Sloane,
until 1733 when he took up an appointment as Professor of
Botany at the St Petersburg Academy. It had been hoped that he
would participate in the Kamchatkan Expedition organized by
the Academy, but delay in sending his engagement contract led
to Gmelin taking his place. In the event he settled down at St
Petersburg, founding and directing the Academy's Botanical
Garden in 1736. He classified and arranged the Academy's
botanical collections, married the Secretary Schumacher's
daughter, compiled and edited the botanical papers of the
naturalist Messerschmidt's extensive manuscripts, and died
young in 1742.

Having been curator of Sloane's collections for several years,
Amman was ideally qualified to know what Russian items would
be most welcomed. It is not possible to do justice to him here, but
fortunately the evidence is in his lengthy correspondence with
Sloane, Collinson, Massey, Catesby, Dillenius, Linnaeus and
other botanists, and is located at the Royal Society, the British

Library and the Bodleian Library.[13] In the course of eight years, Amman sent Sloane and other correspondents hundreds of dried plants, seeds, minerals and many more natural history objects from all over the Russian dominions, and China too, penning a host of information about the progress of the Kamchatkan Expedition, Russian ethnography and, of course, natural history on the broadest scale. From his lively descriptions of the items he sent Sloane, most of them can be traced in the Sloane Manuscripts catalogues of the several departmental libraries at the Natural History Museum, South Kensington, at the British Museum itself, and at the Museum of Mankind, Burlington Gardens, where its ethnographic collections are kept.

John Bell also gave Sloane several items from China and Siberia, not all of them connected with natural history. Of special interest is the 'large tooth, or mammon's horn' which he presented to the collector. There is a detailed entry about it in one of Sloane's catalogues.[14] Sloane contributed a memoir on the subject to the French Academy of Science's *Histoire* for 1727, and several related papers appeared in the Royal Society's *Philosophical Transactions*, one of the most significant being by the eminent anatomist William Hunter who in 1768 pointed out that, whereas Sloane considered Bell's Siberian 'tooth' belonged to an elephant, it, unlike any elephant's tusk he had ever seen, was twisted, which of course supports the case that it came from a mammoth.[15] Incidentally, under the terms of his will Sir Hans Sloane, the first British scientist to be elected honorary member of the St Petersburg Academy, devised that his huge collection should be offered, third choice, for sale to Russia. Instead they were purchased by an Act of Parliament of 1753 and resulted in the foundation of the British Museum in 1759.

The Library of the Royal College of Physicians in Edinburgh has been in continuous existence for over three centuries and is the largest medical library in Scotland. An indexed inventory of the College's muniments provides references, among other documents, to petitions and applications by doctors wishing to be admitted fellows, and their diplomas. Many doctors who had studied medicine at Edinburgh University before working in Russia became fellows of the College. Thus, the petitions on behalf of James Grieve in 1753 and North Vigor in 1755, taken together with their respective diplomas for the same years, shed new light on their medical training and their Russian careers.[16] The information may be supplemented by the College's minutes, a typescript of which is available at the National Library of Scotland.[17] Grieve is best known as the first person to translate Krasheninnikov's pioneering book about Kamchatka into English; it was published in 1764, five years after it appeared in Russian.[18] The importance of Krasheninnikov's work has been stressed by Alexander Vucinich, in his *Science in Russian Culture*, itself a useful introduction to Russian natural history scholarship which forms part of the present study.[19] That Dr North Vigor also interested himself in Russian botany is seen by his owning the first two volumes of Gmelin's influential work *Flora Sibirica* (the four volumes were published between 1747 and 1769) which are in the Wellcome Library.

Peter Collinson, a merchant, member of the Royal Society of London and one of Britain's most distinguished botanists, took an active interest in Russian natural history, helped by his worldwide contacts and correspondence. The *Hortus Collinsonianus*, compiled by L.W. Dillwyn in 1843 from the catalogue of Collinson's garden and other books, contains many details about Russian plants which he received from Amman, Dr James Mounsey and one of the Demidovs.[20] Of greater importance, however, are Peter Collinson's two commonplace books in the library of the Linnean Society. In them is a very informative letter, dated 23 February 1745, from Gmelin about Russian botany, the 'true Rhubarb' (the medicinal rhubarb plant), exchanging seeds for the Academy's garden, and zoology; another letter, written to Collinson by the Scottish surgeon John Cook in Astrakhan on 10 June 1744, giving detailed anatomical replies to Collinson's queries about the beluga, or sturgeon, and the alleged medical properties of the stone often found in it; and part of another letter, dated 11 July 1744, from Cook to Dr Ribeiro Sanches, a Portuguese physician at the Russian capital well known to medical historians, who evidently forwarded it to his correspondent Collinson.[21]

The main part of Cook's letter to Sanches was read on 9 January 1746 by Peter Collinson at the Royal Society. The first half deals with different sorts of natural salts found around

Astrakhan and a specimen of Persian borax, a white salt containing boron, sent by Cook to Sanches who dispatched it to Collinson, who showed it to the Society's members present. The second half is a succinct account of how caviar is prepared from the beluga whale on the Volga near Astrakhan. A few days later, on 15 January, Collinson produced, according to the brief entry in the Society's *Journal Book*, a sample of white naptha sent over by Ribeiro Sanches, and gave an account of it.[22] The full text, surviving at the Wellcome Library, confirms that it was John Cook who sent the original naphtha specimens to Sanches in St Petersburg. Grouped with this letter is another one, dated St Petersburg, 12 April 1746, from Jonas Hanway to Revd John Forster, chaplain to the Earl of Hyndford, British Envoy to Russia. Here again, the substance of Hanway's letter owes much to Cook's testimony about the medicinal qualities of white naphtha and about the so-called 'Everlasting Fire' worshipped by a religious sect in the Baku area.[23]

The Linnean collections—a valuable source of knowledge of Russian botany—deserve a mention. James Edward Smith, an opulent young man from Norwich who had been studying medicine at Edinburgh University, happened to be breakfasting with Sir Joseph Banks, President of the Royal Society, in London at the very time when Banks had been offered the purchase of the whole of the Linnean collections for 1,000 guineas upon the death of the younger Linnaeus at the end of 1783. Catherine the Great made unlimited offers but was pre-empted by Smith who became the first President of the Linnean Society of London which he founded in 1788.

Both Linnaeus senior, who died in 1778, and his son received very considerable amounts of Russian and Siberian plants which are still in Linnaeus's huge herbarium today. An idea of its richness is conveyed by Prince Gregorii Demidov who wrote in a letter dated 15 May 1750 of his collection of over 800 plants which he had sent to Linnaeus for naming, with permission to keep duplicates. Among them were Steller's from Kamchatka, Gerber's from Astrakhan and the river Don, and Lerche's from Persia. Fortunately the history of the Russian contributions has been traced to some extent by Spencer Savage, who compiled a catalogue of the Linnean herbarium, and by the writer Bobrov who, in a book about Linnaeus, devotes a whole chapter to correspondence between Russians and the Swedish botanist.[24] Linnaeus's correspondence itself is enormous and runs into many volumes, with the writers' names alphabetically arranged. Some, but by no means all of the letters from Russia have been published in English, Swedish and Russian works. For example, *A Selection of the Correspondence of Linnaeus and Other Naturalists* by Sir James Edward Smith covers five letters written by Amman at St Petersburg between 1736 and 1740, while Lipskii's book on the St Petersburg Botanical Garden contains thirteen letters from its Swedish-born director Falk, written between 1763 and 1768.[25]

As well as Gregorii Demidov's letter, the Linnean correspondence includes: nine letters from his son Paul, who studied under Linnaeus for a while; nine also from Johann Lerche, John Cook's colleague, written between 1764 and 1774 (vol. 9, fols 88–113); three from the famous naturalist Pallas to Linnaeus senior and junior, 1777 to 1783 (vol. 9, fols 378–92); one from Count Razumovskii, dated St Petersburg, 23 September 1754 (vol. 12, fol. 103); and another from Dr Kruse in Moscow, 7 May 1763 (vol. 8, fols 301–3).

Kruse was a close colleague of James Mounsey, a Scottish surgeon who married a relative of Dr James Grieve. At the close of the Russian campaign against the Swedes, in which he participated as a senior military surgeon, Mounsey wrote about surgical and botanical matters to Linnaeus from Nyköping on 29 March 1744. His letter also survives among the Linnean correspondence.[26]

As this survey is primarily concerned with archival sources, I shall not sketch Mounsey's career except in so far as is necessary in the context. Suffice it to say, that as a result of several papers which he contributed from Russia to the *Philosophical Transactions*, he was elected a fellow of the Royal Society on 8 March 1750. In many instances, however, it is not enough to accept the published papers at their face value. An illustration is Mounsey's account of a case of lead poisoning which appeared in the *Philosophical Transactions* for 1757.[27] If the original of Mounsey's paper is examined, as is possible in many cases from an indexed reference in the Royal Society's Archives, one finds the words 'Print no more of this paper'. A large part of Mounsey's paper has been omitted, much of it theoretical but also of interest because he describes some of his own experiments in medical electricity.

Sometimes, when the Royal Society's Journal Books fail to cover presentations to the Society, the volumes of donations will clarify the issue. A case in point is a sheet headed 'The Report of a Committee appointed to examine a large Collection of Stones, &c.—sent as a Present to the Royal Society from Siberia by Count S.' and read on 22 January 1761. The gift consisted of 260 valuable items which James Parsons, Peter Collinson, Henry Baker and Emanuel Mendes da Costa catalogued. Who was the 'Count S'? The answer is supplied by the list of donors to the Society: he was Count Ivan Shuvalov, Grand Chamberlain to Elizabeth, who gave the collection on 11 December 1760 (having been elected a fellow in 1758).[28]

An exceptionally rich archival source of Anglo-Russian medical and natural history is to be found in Henry Baker's literary and philosophical correspondence held at the John Rylands University of Manchester Library. Baker, a naturalist and fellow of the Royal Society, initiated a correspondence with James Mounsey in Russia during 1747 and they continued to exchange letters for twenty-three years, almost until Mounsey's death at Edinburgh in 1773. This correspondence, which includes Baker's draft copies to Mounsey, is invaluable for the light it sheds on what interested the British in Russia and for amplifying the half dozen papers Mounsey contributed to the *Philosophical Transactions*. Not only this, but it also shows that Mounsey responded by providing Baker and other Royal Society members with large and varied consignments of every conceivable form of Russian natural history, often with descriptions attached.[29]

James Mounsey also has the distinction of being awarded the gold medal of the Royal Society of Arts for introducing to Britain the seed of the 'true Rhubarb', the medicinal *Rheum palmatum* L., which he had sent to Baker from Russia in 1761. On his return to Scotland in 1762 he had given Sir Alexander Dick, President of the Royal College of Physicians of Edinburgh, a packet of the seed which was passed on to John Hope, a fellow of the College, Professor of Botany and *materia medica* at the University, and superintendent of the Royal Botanic Garden, who successfully raised the plant and published an account of it in the *Philosophical Transactions* for 1763. For this service Mounsey was elected an honorary fellow of the College in November 1762.[30]

This much is common knowledge. However, further details have emerged recently which illustrate, at one and the same time, the advantages of consulting the reports of the National Register of Archives, and the hazards of relying too much upon them. The National Register of Archives was established in 1945 by the Royal Commission on Historical Manuscripts to pool information about manuscript resources for British history outside the Public Records. In its search room—and, of course, at the National Register of Archives for Scotland at the Scottish Record Office—there is a thick file entitled 'Scottish Record Office. Subject Source Lists'. These include 'Medicine', 'Science and Technology' and 'Russia', with a breakdown of private muniments, alphabetically arranged under these headings. These lists are constantly being updated. In 'Source List no. 22. Russia' there are brief details about letters that Mounsey and Bell wrote to Hope concerning medicinal rhubarb, with further mention of an excerpt of Pallas's letter to Lord Hope on the subject dated 18 August 1777. The final reference number and page refers to a supposedly more detailed description under the survey of records made by the National Register of Archives (Scotland) in the 1960s. This survey may be consulted in London, Edinburgh, or elsewhere, but so far as the Hope Papers in the D. and J. H. Campbell W.S. Collection are concerned the description is fairly general, in no great detail and not particularly comprehensive. A further letter from John Bell to Hope in the same 'rhubarb' bundle only turned up after interest had been taken in the two others.[31] Nor is any mention made of important material connected with Russia in the 'asafoetida' bundle—the medicinal plant which Matthew Guthrie, another Scottish physician in Russia, introduced to Professor Hope, having obtained the seed from Pallas.

Among the Hope Papers are his notebooks of persons who attended his botany and *materia medica* lectures and notes of those whom he invited to supper. Names, dates and payments are all written down. One comes across the names of doctors who went to Russia, such as Baron Dimsdale, Matthew Guthrie, John Grieve, John Rogerson, Alexander Wylie (who figures in

Tolstoi's *War and Peace*), and Alexander Crichton, as well as those of Russian students at the University: Bakhmetev and Pishchekov. It is possible that these student lists will help to fill gaps in the medical matriculation records kept in the Special Collections at Edinburgh University Library. The archives of the Royal Botanic Garden, Edinburgh, itself, have no Russian correspondence prior to the late nineteenth century.[32]

The same National Register of Archives' file of subject source lists at the Scottish Record Office describes a collection of Rogerson letters deposited on indefinite loan. They are associated with Dr John Rogerson who for many years was a physician at the Russian court. From a medical and natural historical angle the letters are not particularly informative, although they mention some of his former colleagues in Russia and there is a memorial of his career.[33] Of much greater significance are three Rogerson letters to John Clerk of Eldin, among the Clerk of Penicuik Muniments. They prove beyond doubt that John Rogerson played a far more active role in promoting Anglo-Russian natural history than previously thought. From the first two letters, written at St Petersburg in 1772 and 1773, it transpires that Rogerson sent his correspondent parcels of seeds from pine, larch, cedar, barley and buckwheat, from all over Russia, for Clerk to cultivate, together with some Ukrainian seeds for Hope's use. In the third letter, which is undated but relates to 1783, Rogerson writes:

> I have sent for Dr. Hope some rare and I believe new seeds that the Empress has received last week from Siberia collected by a Professor Laxman who has been employed during last year in examining a hitherto inexplored District of that Region. Dr. Grieve has promised to transmit them to Edinburgh without loss of time that they may be immediately planted—The same Collector has likewise sent several new Shrubs—they are in the hands of the Empress English Gardiner—I will try what I can make of them if they succeed.

In the same letter Rogerson explained that, at Dr Walker's request, he had dispatched in the autumn of 1782 'upwards of an hundred Specimens of Russian and Siberian Ores' supplied to him by Pallas. He even proposed opening a correspondence between Pallas and Walker.[34] John Walker was Regius Professor of Natural History at Edinburgh University, a very enthusiastic botanist and mineralogist and one of the organizers of the Royal Society of Edinburgh founded in 1783. A correspondence between him and Pallas might have been as fruitful as that between Pallas and the English naturalist Thomas Pennant.

There is some useful background information about Drs Rogerson, Mounsey, Guthrie and Grieve in the eight or so letters of correspondence in 1960 between Major H. M. Heyder and the then Curator of Historical Records at the Scottish Record Office.[35]

John Grieve, who may not in fact have delivered Rogerson's letter to John Clerk in 1783, is an engaging figure. Educated at Edinburgh University, he saw five years as a military doctor in the Voronezh Division before he returned to Britain on health grounds. Encouraged by Joseph Black, under whom he had studied medicine, Grieve wrote a paper, an excellent, pioneering one of its kind, on the medical applications of kumis, or fermented mare's milk, based on first-hand experience, and Black read it at the Royal Society of Edinburgh.[36] On the strength of this communication, Grieve was elected a non-resident fellow in the Physical Class (with James Walker as the Secretary) on 26 January 1784—the same day as Pallas. It was the first meeting since the inaugural one in June 1783 at which an election took place. Joseph Black's correspondence at Edinburgh University Library has two letters from John Grieve which expand on what he had written about kumis, whereas one of these and an earlier one written from Paris, though adding nothing to knowledge of Russia, contain exceptionally good accounts of ballooning, mesmerism and the latest French experiments in chemistry, all of absorbing interest to Black.[37]

Grieve settled down to a lucrative medical practice in London, joining numerous societies before ending his days as Court Physician in Russia. He was elected a fellow of the Royal Society on 22 May 1794, as 'a gentleman well versed in various branches of natural knowledge.'[38] Generally speaking, it pays to examine certificates of Royal Society members as they frequently supply handy data.

Matthew Guthrie was a contemporary of Grieve and Rogerson. In 1778 he was appointed Chief Physician to the Imperial Land Cadet Corps of Nobles at St Petersburg, a position which he held until his death in 1807. He corresponded with Priestley, John Howard, James Hutton and Joseph Black. Like Mounsey, he too contributed several papers to the *Philosophical Transactions* on Russian medical and natural history, and was elected a Fellow of the Royal Society on 11 April 1782. The late Jessie Sweet wrote an excellent paper about Guthrie as a gemmologist, supplying with it an annotated bibliography of his printed works and manuscripts. However, even she did not come across an un-indexed copy at the Royal Society of a letter which Guthrie wrote to Dr Maxwell Garthshore in 1783 about Catherine's tour of the Crimea, attached to which, and possibly from the same source, are the instructions issued in 1785 to Joseph Billings for his expedition to north-east Asia, and to Eugene Patrin as its naturalist and historiographer.[39]

Many archives have unidentified manuscripts, and the Royal Society is no exception. Among its 'Classified Papers' is a description, in Latin, of the Surinam toad, with references to an accompanying figure. It can be identified because it is in the same hand as 'A Letter written to Esque Van de Bembe by Monsr. N. Witsen' from Amsterdam on 28 February 1690 about the toad, accompanied by a large pencil drawing of it. The writing also matches that of other unattributed so-called 'Classified Papers' which prove to be descriptions by Witsen, in Dutch, of Tobol'sk and the Samoyeds, together with his history of Muscovy.[40] They may even be preliminary sketches for Witsen's classic work, *Noord – en Oost Tartarije*, published at Amsterdam in 1705, although this would require careful checking.

Both Guthrie and John Grieve became members of the Society for Promoting Natural History. The Society originated in October 1782, replacing the short-lived Society of Entomologists of London and lasting until May 1822, when its funds, books and collections were transferred to the Linnean Society. Grieve was elected on 24 May 1790 and played an active part in its proceedings. Archdeacon Robert Nares, who has an entry in the *Dictionary of National Biography* and who was present when Grieve was proposed, donated to the British Museum in 1797 a slab of malachite from the Urals which is still displayed. Guthrie and Count Anhalt, President of the Free Economic Society at St Petersburg, were simultaneously elected members of the Society for Promoting Natural History on 12 March 1792. Anhalt sent the Society a present of two volumes of Pallas's sumptuous work, *Flora Rossica*, in 1793. Guthrie's letter of thanks survives: in it he offers members a select collection of Russian minerals, listed in an attached note, for £80. The Society's records are now in good shape and filed at the Linnean Society which has a very good card index system as well as printed catalogues of its holdings.[41]

Four British doctors and surgeons in Russia were elected to the Medical Society of London, the oldest surviving medical society in Britain, founded by John Coakley Lettsom, the Quaker physician, in 1773. For some reason the Society's minute books do not record Guthrie's election, but the second volume of its *Memoirs* for 1784 lists him, while the fourth volume contains a letter from him. Dr John Rogerson is also listed as a member, and his son and namesake, elected on 30 April 1792, played an active role on the Society's committees.[42] Another valuable member was Dr Jonathan Rogers who became Physician-General to the Russian navy in 1803 and published a *Pharmacopaea Navalis Rossicae* in 1806.[43] Jesse Foot, who also has an entry in the *Dictionary of National Biography*, served at St Petersburg for a while. Like Guthrie, he was an accredited member of the Corporation of Surgeons of London. He was elected to the Society for Promoting Natural History on the same day as Benjamin Franklin and Dr William Withering of *digitalis* fame.[44] Finally, it is noteworthy that the Russian physician Dr Francis Boutatz was awarded the Society's Fothergillian gold medal on 16 February 1791 for his paper on the medical effects of phosphorus.[45] When he returned to Russia he helped to spread Jenner's doctrines. Some 45 per cent of the Society's printed books have been deposited at the Wellcome Library—the remainder were purchased at Sotheby's for Toronto University Library in 1967. The Wellcome Library, which acquired the Society's tracts in 1984, also has card indexes, arranged according to chronology, post-1850 publications, and serial and tracts.

Between 1785 and 1801 Matthew Guthrie, a prolific correspondent, penned eight letters to Sir Joseph Banks, President of the Royal Society, all on the subject of minerals or other forms of Russian natural history.[46] They make instructive as well as entertaining reading, and are summarized in the large volume of *The Banks Letters, a Calendar of the Manuscript Correspondence of Sir Joseph Banks*, which is an invaluable guide to Banks's colossal correspondence in the British Library, the Royal Society, the Natural History Museum, South Kensington, and in the Royal Botanic Garden Library at Kew. Much correspondence from or concerning Russia is included, with brief but useful biographical details about the correspondents.[47]

There are also two monographs by Guthrie of considerable interest in the British Library's Department of Manuscripts. The first, 'A supplementary tour through the countries on the Black Sea', is interleaved with lively accounts of the plague in Russia, surgeon James Wylie's views on 'yellow' fever, or typhoid, and so on.[48] The second is a companion volume, dating to the beginning of the nineteenth century. It bears the somewhat daunting title: 'Natural history of the Taurida containing a sketch of the geology, orography, zoology, ornithology, ichthyology, entomology, mineralogy, and botany, of that peninsula with practical remarks on each, showing their uses in common life, and the advantages the inhabitants might receive by attending to them'. Guthrie's manuscript comprises a mass of information on all aspects of Crimean natural history. He intends the work to be popular, accessible and factual, in contrast to a book written by Pallas on the same subject which, Guthrie claims, is far too erudite, specialized and costly, and fails to contribute any fresh scientific knowledge. In general, Guthrie succeeds with his aims despite the discursive nature of his writing. As an example, he describes forty-six Crimean medicinal plants in an interesting way, detailing their therapeutic application with much wit and vivacity. He manages to impart many details about their history and culture, without being heavy-handed, retaining a critical approach to their uses in medicine. Much of Guthrie's own medical philosophy is injected into his 'Natural history of the Taurida'. In particular he attacks exaggerated claims to the healing properties of natural remedies which, he considers, would do little harm to gullible John Bull, but for the danger 'in trusting to inactive remedies in serious diseases, and losing precious time which might be employed to the advantage of the sick'.[49]

By any standards Matthew Guthrie's creative output was enormous, both published and unpublished. Taken together they constitute a remarkably varied and representative picture of Anglo-Russian medical science and natural history spanning some thirty years—not to mention his writings on physics, the arts, and industry.

Just as Linnaeus's herbarium is at the Linnean Society, so too is Pallas's very extensive collection, all forty-one boxes of it, at the Herbarium of the Department of Botany of the Natural History Museum. The whole of it is expected to be sorted by 1988. The specimens are well preserved, but many of them lack data.

The Wellcome Library has a large number of autograph letters, including five from Pallas. Although these autograph letters are listed alphabetically, under the writers' names, at the end of a printed volume of the Library's manuscripts, no further details are given. However, card indexes of the letters at the Wellcome Institute provide fuller information, and a comprehensive catalogue of the collection of over 100,000 of the autograph letters is being prepared.[50]

Three of Pallas's letters were written from Russia. The first, dated December 1779, was addressed to the naturalist Patrin who was travelling to Kolyvan and Barnaul from where, with Pallas's encouragement, he would make scientific expeditions. The letter provides direct evidence of Patrin's botanical and mineralogical pursuits. It shows that Pallas, who had used his influence to secure Patrin's election as a corresponding member of the Academy, took a great deal of personal interest in his protégé's activities. The second letter from Pallas gives fulsome thanks to the French Academy of Sciences for electing him a foreign member in 1790, while the third letter, written at Pallas's home at Simferopol' in the Crimea at the beginning of 1803, covers such topics as the Academy's Botanical Garden and *rheum palmatum*.[51]

Also among the Wellcome's Autograph Letters Collection are forty-seven letters which Leonhard Euler wrote between 1746 and 1757 from Berlin to Caspar Wettstein, chaplain and librarian to the Prince of Wales and then, upon Frederick's death in 1751, to the Dowager Princess.[52] They are the originals, all in French, Euler's own copies being retained by the Archives of the USSR Academy of Sciences. They have been partly published. At the time when they were written Euler was very active transforming the Berlin Society of Sciences into the Académie Royale des Sciences et des Belles Lettres de Berlin, supervising its observatory and botanical garden while at the same time managing the publication of calendars and maps.[53] Euler provides Wettstein, who was elected a fellow of the Royal Society in 1754, with much information about his own works and research, his connections with the St Petersburg Academy and its German-born members, the second Kamchatkan expedition (under Behring), and the Virginian seeds and plants that he obtained from his friend Peter Collinson.

An outstanding collection in the Department of Manuscripts at the British Library is the correspondence of Emanuel Mendes da Costa, the naturalist and, more specifically, mineralogist who had helped to secure James Mounsey's election to the Royal Society. It comprises eleven volumes of his letters, alphabetically arranged, with the copies of his replies—altogether 2,487 autographs spanning the fifty-year period from 1737 to 1787. There are several links with Russia. One of them is a letter from Gerhard Friedrich Müller, Secretary of the St Petersburg Academy of Sciences, written in June 1759 to thank Da Costa for sending a copy of his book, the *Natural History of Fossils*, published in 1757. There is a copy of Da Costa's reply dated 16 April 1762, but it was never sent.[54]

One of the most interesting items in these volumes, from an Anglo-Russian viewpoint, is Da Costa's correspondence during 1786 with Revd Yakov Smirnov, who for sixty years was chaplain to the Russian Embassy in London.[55] It concerns an order placed with Smirnov by an unnamed correspondent in Russia, about June 1786, specifying minerals for a natural history cabinet and 'an exact copy of Mr Da Costa's 23.26. & 27. Lectures on Mineralogy with his Catalogue belonging to his Course'. On 24 June Da Costa sent Smirnov a list of the minerals ordered, together with their prices and a copy of his lectures. At the end of his letter he wrote 'This parcel I assure you consists of Curious Scientific Minerals not perhaps to be procured from any single Cabinet in England'. Further correspondence followed before Da Costa delivered the minerals in person to Smirnov on 18 July. Meanwhile Smirnov's correspondent in Russia had supplied another list of desiderata which Smirnov passed on to Da Costa at the end of July. On this occasion very extensive numbers of shells, fossils and minerals, 'not small, but fit for my Cabinet', were requested to be sent as soon as possible.

Within a remarkably short space of time Da Costa, on 7 September, forwarded to Smirnov a catalogue, with prices, for all three categories, hailing from Britain, Germany, Hungary, Italy, China and the East and West Indies. A note at the end of the correspondence says that what Da Costa could procure of 'these natural curiosities' were sent by ship to St Petersburg on 14 September 1786.[56] If one looks up under Smirnov's name, in the volume *Natural History Manuscript Resources in the British Isles*, one discovers that the archives of the Geological Society of London has a copy of Da Costa's book, *Natural History of Fossils*, of 1757, interleaved and with the words 'Remarks and alterations made by Mr. da Costa, the author, and copied in the year 1781 by James Smirnove'. Apparently there are relatively few associations, but it suggests that Smirnov attended Da Costa's lectures and was suitably impressed.

By now many people have read Carol Urness's attractively produced little book, entitled *A Naturalist in Russia*, about the correspondence between Pallas and the English naturalist Thomas Pennant.[57] But not everyone has come across an extremely handy reference work called *The Manuscript Papers of British Scientists 1600–1940*.[58] It is one of the Royal Commission on Historical Manuscripts' series of Guides to Sources for British History, based on the National Register of Archives. It resulted from an enquiry instituted by a joint committee of the Commission and the Royal Society on scientific and technical records, set up in 1966. The preface refers to the guide to manuscript resources in the British Isles, already recommended (see note 1), and to the work of R. M. Macleod and J. R. Friday, *Archives of British Men of Science* (1972, microfilm)—an effort to trace the descendants of some 3,000 scientists of the nineteenth and twentieth centuries, in a search for their surviving papers.

There are several leads to be followed up in the *Manuscript Papers of British Scientists*. For instance, a reference to a Da Costa letter book among the Pennant manuscripts at the Warwickshire County Record Office (TP 408) and a glance at the letters of 1760 in it reveals that the Demidov brothers praised Pennant's collection when they visited him at Downing, Flintshire, in the summer of 1759. And according to the County Archivist, there are also references to Pallas and the Demidovs elsewhere in the Pennant papers. There are letters relating to Pallas from Anna Blackburne in 1778, from E. W. Boothe in 1792, Zimmerman in 1783 and from William Coxe in 1798. Pennant's ornithological notes include an extract from Pallas on catching geese in flight, and there are also printed articles of his in French and Latin.[59]

As one might expect, many Russian minerals have found their way into the British Museum's natural history collections over the years. Pallas's celebrated 'native iron', or meteorite, for instance, is still on display at the Natural History Museum, having been presented by the Imperial Academy of Sciences at St Petersburg in 1776.[60] In 1799 the British Museum acquired from the eminent chemist Charles Hatchett an important collection of minerals, including a fine set from Count Apollon de Musin-Pushkin, the Russian senator and antiquary.[61] The Department of Mineralogy has two manuscript lists of these Siberian minerals. The first one gives the names and district where they are found, while the second list names the 161 items—less numbers 31 to 49 which are missing.[62] In addition to Hatchett, Count Apollon corresponded with Joseph Banks between 1800 and 1806, sending from Nizhnii Novgorod and the Caucasus minerals for Banks and Hatchett and Siberian or Caucasian plants for Banks.[63]

Finally, to refer to fossils, Banks corresponded in 1803 with Nikolai Novosil'tsev, President of the Russian Academy of Sciences, requesting him to convey to the Emperor Alexander I his thanks for his appreciation for Banks's assistance in purchasing sheep and cattle for export to Russia, in the same way that he had helped to send plants from Kew to Catherine II in 1795.[64] He accepted his offer from the Imperial Museum of any spare 'bones, teeth, Sculls or any part of the vast animals found Fossil in Siberia ... '.[65] Novosil'tsev replied that he would be glad to accommodate Banks and was now sending the bones of the various animals by his servant, including those 'which are commonly called Bones of the Mamouth (or Mamont) ... ', 'but I must observe,' he added, 'that our Naturalists conceive them to be Elephants Bones and not those of any other Species, only that they are of an enormous Size, and such as do not at present exist ... '.[66]

The Palaeological Library of the Natural History Museum has

a manuscript of the fossil bones presented to Banks in 1803 by Alexander I, including bones or horns of elephants, rhinoceros, sheep and the saiga antelope. However, at a committee meeting held in 1813, Charles König the mineralogist and keeper, having reported that the 'lower Jaw only of the Fossil Head of an Extinct Species of Elephant, presented by Sir Joseph Banks some years ago to the Museum, is now extant', he was asked to enquire at the 'College of Surgeons whether the Upper Part of the said Head has been delivered by mistake with the Articles formerly sent there'.[67] Nothing further was heard, so that one must presume that it, too, like Bell's 'tusk', went the way of all flesh!

From 1807 onwards, natural history items proliferate, sent from Russia to the Linnean Society, the Geological Society, the Royal Botanic Garden, Kew, the Royal Horticultural Society, and many other organizations, but I hope I have shown that British archives also contain Anglo-Russian medical and natural historical material of much interest for the period under review and that the subject justifies its own place in the overall survey of Russian manuscript resources in the United Kingdom.[68]

Notes

1. Natural history materials are described in *Natural History Manuscript Resources in the British Isles*, edited by D. R. Bridson *et al.* (London and New York, 1980). Regrettably there is no equivalent to British medical manuscript archives.

2. See J. H. Appleby, 'British Doctors in Russia, 1657–1807: their Contribution to Anglo-Russian Medical and Natural History' (unpublished Ph.D. Thesis, University of East Anglia, 1978), pp. 6–7, 374.

3. William Munk, *The Roll of the Royal College of Physicians of London*, 3 vols (London, 1878).

4. Guildhall Library, MS 8286, draft bill, 1634–5, and John H. Appleby, 'Ivan the Terrible to Peter the Great: British formative influence on Russia's medico-apothecary system', *Medical History*, 27 (1983), 293–4.

5. Guildhall Library, MSS 8200–94, Apothecaries; MSS 11, 741/1–10, Russia Company; MS 11,192:B, Chapel Register.

6.   L. Loewenson, 'The Works of Robert Boyle and *The Present State of Russia* by Samuel Collins (1671)', *The Slavonic and East European Review*, 33 (1955), 470–85; *The Works of the Honourable Robert Boyle*, 5 (London, 1772), pp. 639–42, Collins to Boyle, Archangel, 1 September 1663, and Vologda, 20 November 1663; Appleby thesis, pp. 10–23.

7.   N. Novombergskii, *Materialy po istorii meditsiny v Rossii*, 5 vols and supplement (Leningrad and Tomsk, 1905–10), nos 154 and 1058.

8.   British Museum (Natural History) (BM (NH)), Library press mark L.MSS.APP; John H. Appleby, 'Robert Erskine—Scottish pioneer of Russian Natural History', *Archives of Natural History*, 10 (1982), 377–98; John H. Appleby, 'Robert Erskine and Archibald Pitcairne—two Scottish Physicians' Outstanding Libraries', *The Bibliotheck*, 11 (1982), 3–16.

9.   Royal Society (RS), Royal Society Letter Book (RSLB), 15, 1712–13 and Journal Book of the Royal Society (JBRS), 19 February 1712/13 and 7 March 1712/13; 'Robert Erskine––Scottish pioneer', pp. 380–2; Appleby thesis, pp. 58–61.

10.   V. I. Lipskii, *Istoricheskii ocherk Imperatorskago S.-Peterburgskago Botanicheskago Sada (1713–1913)* (St Petersburg, 1913); Yakov Chistovich, *Istoriya pervykh meditsinskikh shkol v Rossii* (St Petersburg, 1883).

11.   John Bell, *Travels from St Petersburg in Russia to Diverse Parts of Asia*, 2 vols (Glasgow, 1763).

12.   Scottish Record Office (SRO), Admiral Gordon Papers, GD 24/856, 859.

13.   RS, JBRS and RSLB and 14 photocopies of letters from Sloane to Amman and another, 1730–40, presented by the USSR Academy of Sciences in 1956; see indexes of British Library, Add. MSS; Bodleian Library, MS Sherard 207, fols 33–4. See also for details of Amman's specimens and those from others in Russia, Hermia Newman Clokie, *An Account of the Herbaria of the Department of Botany in the University of Oxford* (Oxford, 1964).

14.   BM (NH), Palaeontological Department Library, MS Sloane Catalogue 50.h.6: *Fishes, birds, eggs, quadrupeds*, no. 1185.

15. Appleby thesis, pp. 119–21, 122–4, 126–7.
16. *Inventory of the Muniments of the Royal College of Physicians of Edinburgh*, pp. 6, 15, 54–5; diplomas nos 11 and 14. See W. J. Robertson, 'A Checklist of the Manuscripts in the Royal College of Physicians of Edinburgh' (submitted for the University of London Diploma in Librarianship, August 1975); National Register of Archives report no. 16015.
17. National Library of Scotland, MS 3439; for Dr North Vigor, see pp. 1085–6.
18. *The History of Kamtschatka and the Kurilski Islands, translated by James Grieve, M.D.* (Gloucester, 1764).
19. Alexander Vucinich, *Science in Russian Culture* (London, 1965), p. 45.
20. *Hortus Collinsonianus. An Account of the Plants Cultivated by the Late Peter Collinson*, edited by L. W. Dillwyn (Swansea, 1843).
21. Linnean Society Library, Peter Collinson's Commonplace Books, 2 vols MS 323 (and microfilm 629); J. G. Gmelin, vol. 1, pp. 15–18; Cook to Collinson, pp. 300–3; Cook to Sanches, extract, pp. 304–7.
22. RS, RSLP, decade 1.438, and JBRS, vol. 19, pp. 14–16 and 185–6.
23. Wellcome Library, Wellcome Autograph Letters, no. 67721, 'An Account of the Naphtha Alba by Mr Peter Collinson' and J. Hanway's letter to Revd Forster; Appleby thesis, pp. 291–304.
24. *A Catalogue of the Linnaean Herbarium*, compiled and annotated by Spencer Savage (London, 1945), pp. vii–viii, and see also Benjamin Daydon-Jackson, *Notes on a Catalogue of the Linnean Herbarium (London, 1922)*, pp. 11–21; E. G. Bobrov, *Karl Linney 1707–1778* (Leningrad, 1970), pp. 232–7.
25. Sir James Edward Smith, *A Selection of the Correspondence of Linnaeus and Other Naturalists* (London, 1821), pp. 191–203; Lipskii, note no. 9, pp. 169–88.
26. Linnean Society of London, Archives, Linnaeus's Correspondence, vol. 10, fol. 276. See Appleby thesis, pp. 174–6, for a rough translation of the Latin text.
27. James Mounsey, 'On the Strange Effects of Some Effervescent Mixtures', *Philosophical Transactions*, 50 (1757),

19–22; RS, RSLP, Decade 111.203 (vol. 24) (2).

28. RS, *Donations to Library and Museum*, vol. 419 (1744–9).

29. John Rylands University of Manchester Library, Henry Baker's Literary and Philosophical Correspondence, vols 3–8; Appleby thesis, pp. 116–74.

30. Appleby thesis, pp. 337–50.

31. SRO, GD 253/144/2/5, 9. John H. Appleby, '"Rhubarb" Mounsey and the Surinam toad—a Scottish Physician–Naturalist in Russia', *Archives of Natural History*, 11 (1982), 142–5. Pallas's letter to Lord Hope would appear to be the prototype for the description of rhubarb by William Coxe in his *Account of the Russian Discoveries between Asia and America* (London, 1780), pp. 334–8. See also my forthcoming article, 'St Petersburg to Edinburgh—Matthew Guthrie's Introduction of Medicinal Plants in the Context of Scottish–Russian Natural History Exchange', *Archives of Natural History* which is largely based on materials in the Hope Papers.

32. SRO, GD 253/144/8/1, 8, 9, 16, 21, 25, 29.

33. SRO, GD 1/620, items 1–35.

34. SRO, GD 18/521.

35. SRO, 'Historical Department Letters 1960. A–J'.

36. John Grieve, 'An Account of the Method of Making a Wine, called by the Tartars Koumiss; with Observations of its Use in Medicine', *Transactions of the Royal Society of Edinburgh*, 1 (1783–5), 178–90; Appleby thesis, pp. 206–12.

37. Edinburgh University Library, Joseph Black's Correspondence, MS Gen. 873/2, fols 171–3, Paris, 11 May 1784; fols 195–6, Hertford, 8 October 1784; MS Gen. 874/4, fols 17–18, London, 8 May 1785.

38. RS, 'Certificates 1784–1800', vol. 4, fol. 230.

39. RS, Misc. MSS, no. 7.60, Guthrie to Garthshore, 23 June 1783 (probably a copy made by Garthshore); in the same hand, 60.1–6, Joseph Billing's instructions; 60.7–9, instructions to Patrin; 60.10–12, in a different hand, French text of the expedition's overall aims.

40. RS, Classified Papers, 36, fols 81–2v; *RSLB*, 2 (1), pp. 184–6; CP 7 (1), 16: Tobol'sk, 17: Samoyeds; and CP 14 (1), 20: history of Muscovy. Appleby, '"Rhubarb" Mounsey', pp. 146–9.

41. Appleby thesis, pp. 219–20, 265–7, 269, 373.
42. Medical Society of London (MSL), Minutes 2 (1790–5); 30 April 1792, 8 March 1793 and 27 January 1794.
43. MSL, Minutes, 1 (1773–16 July 1787): elected in January 1774, present in February but then absent in Russia until 3 November 1778; read a paper on palsy on 12 January 1779, etc.; last present on 2 December 1783.
44. MSL, Minutes, 1: 2 and 16 July 1787.
45. MSL, Minutes of the Council (1799–1809), 19 and 26 January, and 2 and 16 February 1801.
46. British Library, Additional MSS (BL, Add. MSS) 8096 and 8099.
47. *The Banks Letters, a Calendar of the Manuscript Correspondence of Sir Joseph Banks*, edited by Warren R. Dawson (London, 1958).
48. BL, Add. MS 14388, fols 307–11.
49. BL, Add. MS 14389 (1804–5), fols 166–8, 182 etc. See Appleby thesis, pp. 241–2, 246–7, 260–1, 271.
50. *Manuscripts on Medicine and Science in the Wellcome Historical Medical Library*, compiled by S. A. J. Moorat; vol. 2, *Manuscripts written after 1650 A.D.* (London, 1973), pp. 1409–59. The Curator of Western Manuscripts at the Wellcome Institute writes (26 April 1984) that preparation has begun of a supplement to this work which will include a description of the Wellcome autograph letters.
51. Wellcome Library, Autograph Letters, 67129, Pallas to Patrin, St Petersburg, 25 December 1779 ('Recue a Barnaul le 24 fevr. 1780'); 66597, St Petersburg, 4 January 1791; 63459, Simferopol', 16 January 1803 (addressee's names not indicated for 66597 and 63459).
52. *Dictionary of Scientific Biography*, edited by C.C. Gillispie, IV (New York, 1971), 467–84, A. P. Yuskevich's entry on Euler.
53. Wellcome Library, Autograph Letters, Euler 48, 8 January 1746 to 26 March 1757.
54. BL, Add. MSS 28,534–44; MS 28,540 (vol. 7), fol. 51: Müller to Da Costa, St Petersburg, 21 June 1759, and Da Costa to Müller, 16 April 1762 (not sent).
55. See A. G. Cross, 'Yakov Smirnov: a Russia Priest of Many Parts', *Oxford Slavonic Papers*, 8 (1975), 37–52.

56. BL, Add. MS 28,542, fols 221–33v; *Natural History Manuscript Resources*, p. 193.

57. *A Naturalist in Russia (Letters from Peter Simon Pallas to Thomas Pennant)*, edited and annotated by Carol Urness (Minneapolis, 1967). Pallas's letters to Pennant are in the James Ford Collection at Minnesota University.

58. *The Manuscript Papers of British Scientists 1600–1940* (London, 1982).

59. Letter, 12 March 1984, from Mr M. W. Farr, County Archivist, Warwickshire County Record Office.

60. *The History of the Collections Contained in the Natural History Departments of the British Museum* (London, 1904), vol. 1, p. 406.

61. Ibid., p. 358.

62. BM (NH), Department of Mineralogy Library. Musin-Pushkin Collection (1799), MS Lists, fols 1–6.

63. BL, Add. MS 8099, fols 92–6, 358; four letters from Musin-Pushkin to Banks.

64. Harold B. Carter, 'Sir Joseph Banks and the Plant Collection from Kew sent to the Empress Catherine II of Russia 1795', *Bulletin of the British Museum (Natural History)*, Historical Series, 4 (1974), 281–385.

65. BM (NH), Botany Department Library, Dawson Turner Collection, vol. 14, fols 31–2, Banks to Novosil'tsev, Soho Square, 7 March 1803.

66. BL, Add. MS 8099, fols 360–2, Novosil'tsev to Banks, St Petersburg, 7 July 1803.

67. BM (NH), Palaeontological Library MSS, 'Fossil and recent Bones presented by Sir Joseph Banks, to whom they were sent by the Emperor of Russia in 1803'.

68. The following article has been published since this paper was given: John H. Appleby, 'John Grieve's Correspondence with Joseph Black and some Contemporaneous Russo-Scottish Medical Intercommunication', *Medical History*, 29 (1985), 401–13.

Material on Russian Political Emigrants in British Archives 1850–1917

JOHN SLATTER

It is only seventy years since you could have walked in many parts of London and thought yourself in some quarter of a Russian city.[1] The East End of London, of course, was inhabited by many Russians, Jews and non-Jews, but other parts of the capital were also the haunts of the numerous Russian population.[2] Hammersmith and Chiswick, for instance, were the abode of Feliks Volkhovskii and David Soskice, and of the Free Russian Press Fund which they helped to run.[3] The German Workers' Education League in Charlotte Street, dubbed the 'Communist Club',[4] provided a meeting-place, while nearby the British Museum Reading Room was full of Russian *intelligenty*—Stepniak, Kropotkin, Bervi-Flerovskii, Burtsev[5] and Lenin, to name but a few—some unable to communicate with its ever patient staff except in broken French, and that despite several decades of unbroken residence in Britain.

There was also a Free Russian Library just off Bishopsgate, on the edge of the City of London, which was one small room smelling strongly of Russian newsprint and tobacco, thronged with emigrants and immigrants alike who had come to read the latest controversy in *tolstye zhurnaly* published in the land they had, for their various reasons, rejected. The London Library in respectable St James's Square, though in every other respect a contrast to the library just described, was in the charge of the

This research was aided by grants from the University of Durham Staff Travel and Research Fund.

Russophile C. T. Hagberg-Wright and no doubt also contained its contingent of refugees 'from the other shore'.[6] Outside London, the Leylands district of Leeds was a smaller version of the East End; additionally, Tolstoyan colonies with a fair sprinkling of Russians were established first near Southend and then, in 1900, outside Bournemouth, in Hampshire, on the south coast.

In principle, the activity of this teeming population should have left a considerable literary trace: around fifty Russian-language magazines and newspapers[7] and a few hundred Russian-language books and pamphlets[8] which provide a sampling of the patchwork of ideologies among the emigration, as do the frequent contributions it made to the British labour press— *Labour Leader, Justice* and others—and to the English-language magazines it sponsored, such as *Free Russia, In Darkest Russia, The Anglo-Russian* and *Russian Correspondence.*

The position is quite different with regard to archives, however. The initial conservation of personal archives is at best a hazardous business, dependent on the presence of factors such as a loving wife and adoring children, ownership of a large attic, etc. If these factors are absent, then natural entropy and the particularly disturbing effect of world events in this century will do the work of scattering or destroying the most carefully amassed papers. Russian intellectuals were generally conscious of how they might appear to posterity and played a large role in recording the early history of the liberation movement: journals like *Byloe, Minuvshiya gody, Golos minuvshago* and *Katorga i ssylka* bulged every month with memoirs and documentary material about the revolutionary movement by its participants. Many of these participants were also therefore careful to ensure that the archive of their correspondence and other working materials was well-kept and up-to-date. If surprisingly little of this type of material has remained here in the case of the 'London emigration', we must seek the cause in events outside the control of the emigrants themselves.

For many years, from the revolutions of 1917 to the early 1950s, the history of the non-Bolshevik emigration was largely ignored by those writing in the West. For historians struggling to deal with the Soviet regime, the story of revolutionaries who failed to make a revolution must have seemed largely irrelevant.

Indeed, the only interest in chronicling the movement seems to have come from its survivors, both in the Soviet Former Exiles' and Convicts' Society (*Obshchestvo byvshikh ssylno-poselentsev i polit-katorzhan*) and in the post-revolutionary emigrants' colonies abroad: the Paris Russian Book-lovers' Society (*Obshchestvo lyubitelei russkoi knigi*) and those around the Prague Russian Historical Archive Abroad (*Russkii zagranichnyi istoricheskii arkhiv*).

It was in this third of a century of obscurity that much of the archival material relating to the British emigration disappeared abroad. A large proportion returned to Russia with its owners after the February Revolution: Kropotkin's archive is one such. Others, although remaining accessible in the West, went to the Prague archive which was seized after the war by an NKVD detachment commanded by the Soviet historian A. A. Sidorov, transported to the USSR and there incorporated into the Central State Archive of the October Revolution (Tsentral'nyi gosudarstvennyi arkhiv Oktyabr'skoi Revolyutsii, TsGAOR):[9] this happened to the archives of L. B. Gol'denberg,[10] N. V. Chaikovskii[11] and E. E. Lazarev. Finally, perhaps the most extensive archive of all, that of Sergei Mikhailovich Kravchinskii (pseud. Stepniak), was sold to the Soviet government by his widow in the mid–1930s, together with a large part of Edward Pease's papers, having been offered to the British Library of Political and Economic Science at a low price and refused for lack of interest.[12]

Still other archives disappeared abroad to places other than the USSR. Feliks Volkhovskii's papers were kept in pristine order by his daughter Vera until, in the 1950s, she sent a large part to the Hoover Institution. On her death, part of the remainder was bought at auction by the Houghton Library of Harvard University, and part by the same Hoover Institution. The International Institute for Social History, Amsterdam, has, among other archives pertinent to the London emigration, those of Valerian Smirnov, P. L. Lavrov's assistant at the Forward Journal Press (*Nabornya zhurnala 'Vpered'*)[13] and of Rudolf Rocker, the German leader of Russian Jewish anarchists in the East End of London before 1914.[14] Columbia University's Archive of Russian and East European History contains a Stepniak-Kravchinskii collection of letters to his wife and to a young actress Emily Willard which somehow came into the possession of M. L. Sabsovich, a Russian revolutionary who emigrated to the USA and formed a Zionist Socialist (*Poale-Zion*) colony outside New York in the 1890s.

There remain four personal archives of Russian revolutionaries in Britain which take on an increased importance because of their very scarcity. They are those of D. V. Soskis (anglicized as Soskice) (1867–1943),[15] A. F. Alad'in (1873–1927), P. A. Sirnis (1882–1918) and G. V. Chicherin (1872–1936).[16] As the Soskice Papers have already been catalogued, it may be best here to survey their contents very broadly. Their interest lies in several qualities. First, their completeness: D. V. Soskice was clearly not a man to throw anything away, and his papers seem to include almost everything retained in the course of a long and active life. Equally, his activities covered several spheres, combining in one lifetime the lives of a political activist, a practising lawyer, a well-known journalist and a businessman. Second, their spanning of, on the one hand, British life where, as a member by marriage of the Hueffer family, he had an entrée to British intellectual circles (his brother-in-law was Ford Madox Ford, author and editor of the *New English Review*) and, on the other hand, Russian life both in emigration (he remained in Britain from 1898 to 1943 with short stays in Russia) and at home (his stays there in 1905–6 and 1917 coincided with heightened political activity there, and on the second occasion he was appointed A. F. Kerenskii's political secretary). Third, Soskice's political activities themselves ranged through a wide spectrum of ideologies. He was for some time in the 1880s a *narodovolets* (supporter of the People's Will party), then in the 1890s became a legal Marxist, and by the 1900s had become associated with the Agrarian-Socialist League, a sort of political 'decompression chamber' for members of the Free Russian Press Fund before their entry into the Social Revolutionary Party. Before and during the Great War he practised as a lawyer in the Russian Law Bureau then operating in Lincoln's Inn Fields.

Soskice's papers therefore reflect this long and varied life. From the 1890s, there is his correspondence with major figures like G. V. Plekhanov,[17] P. N. Milyukov, F. V. Volkhovskii and N. V. Chaikovskii: from the 1900s, documents and letters relating to the Society for Popular Lectures in the East End (a group devoted to the education of London's Russian–Jewish working class), the Agrarian-Socialist League, the House of Commons' Parliamentary Russian Committee, the publication of *Free Russia* (the journal of the Society of Friends of Russian Freedom), the visits to Britain of Georgii Gapon in 1905 and of Vera Figner in 1909, and the propagandizing of Russian prisoners-of-war in Japan in 1904–6. There is further correspondence from a later period relating to Soskice's activities in the women's rights cause and the Russian anti-conscription movement during the war, but disappointingly little on Soskice's period in Russia in 1917 as A. F. Kerenskii's political aide, though there is a file of Kerenskii material of a later date. The papers also contain a great deal of probably unique material about post-1917 émigré organizations close to the Social Revolutionary Party.

The Alad'in Papers in the John Rylands University of Manchester Library have not yet been catalogued. They consist of thirty-six small boxes, many of which relate to the post-1917 period or are purely personal letters. Others, perhaps unique, relate to Alad'in's membership of the First Duma (February–June 1906), where he was head of the Peasant Labour Party (boxes 10–12, 15, 16, 19, 20, 25). They contain communications from his constituents and from peasants all over Russia, and would no doubt afford an interesting comparison with that part of the Soskice Papers which deals with Soskice's activities as a barrister concerned with civil rights cases in the Russian courts in 1906–7. Of most interest to students of the British emigration, however, are probably papers collected by Alad'in during an investigation of some of the ramifications of the 1910 Houndsditch murders (boxes 1, 8).

The Leeds Russian Archive is full of most unexpected and interesting items on the Russian emigration to Britain; it also has some fascinating insights relating principally to the Tolstoyans, a topic not covered by other collections. There are, first, papers relating to Aylmer Maude: letters from him to his literary agents G. H. Perris and Charles Cazenove—these have already been catalogued[18]—and letters to him, mainly from Tolstoi's family with a very few, of limited interest unfortunately, from Peter Kropotkin, David Soskice and Paul Vinogradoff. The letters to Maude are on loan to a member of staff of the Russian Studies Department at Leeds University and are at present being catalogued. The second part of the Tolstoyan collection, the Tuckton House Papers, relate more particularly to the emigration. Tuckton House was the place outside Bournemouth where the Tolstoyan colony settled after leaving Purleigh, Essex, in 1900.[19] Up to 1908, the colony and its Free Age Press were run by Tolstoi's amanuensis, V. G. Chertkov, who then returned to Russia leaving Peter Alexander Sirnis ('Sasha') as the colony's secretary until his death in 1918. The Tuckton House Papers contain, in addition to a large number of Free Age editions in both English and Russian, nine correspondence notebooks kept by Sirnis between 1912 and 1918, all but one being already sorted with Sirnis's own index. These detail the affairs of the colony and its gradual decline, especially after the outbreak of the Great War.

Finally, the papers of G. V. Chicherin, usually referred to as the Bridges Adams Papers. After considerable anti-conscription activity in Britain between 1915 and 1917, Chicherin was arrested and kept in Brixton Jail under the Aliens Restriction Act of 1914 before being released into deportation early in 1918. His entire archive, left behind in his garret in Oakley Square, Camden, after his arrest, was kept for him by his political assistant Mrs Mary Jane Bridges Adams.[20] However, if Mrs Bridges Adams hoped to hand the papers back to Chicherin on his release she was disappointed: the British authorities decided to deport Chicherin directly back to Russia without releasing him first here in order to settle his affairs. The two colleagues met briefly in the buffet of King's Cross Station under the watchful eyes of Chicherin's guards before his departure for Newcastle, Norway and revolutionary Russia. Thus the Chicherin archive remained in Britain, and thus it is known as the Bridges Adams Papers.

The papers are a principal source for the history of two organizations, the Russian Political Prisoners' and Exiles' Relief Committee (RPPERC) and the Committee of Delegates of Russian Socialist Groups in London (CoDoRSGiL). The RPPERC was an organization devoted to propagandizing in Britain the plight of Russian political prisoners, collecting donations from the public for the exiles and convicts, and sending the money on to them in Russia. The RPPERC's minutes, accounts and correspondence, together with Chicherin's speeches to its meetings, are all present in the Bridges Adams

Papers.[21] The CoDoRSGiL, whose brochures in English, Russian and Yiddish may be consulted in the British Library Reference Division, was engaged between mid–1916 and late 1917 in resisting the attempt by the British Government to conscript unnaturalized Russians into the British Army.[22] Minutes, accounts and correspondence of the CoDoRSGiL are all in the Bridges Adams Papers. There is also an open Home Office file on the campaign (see note 1) and a closed one on Chicherin's activities which has, however, been shown to some researchers on application.[23] Additionally, the Catherine Marshall papers (the archive of the No-Conscription Fellowship in Cumbria County Archive) tell a related story on the British side of the anti-conscription struggle, with unexpected sidelights on the campaign among Russians. Closed government files on Chicherin's collaborators in the campaign are in many cases still closed (for example Peter Petroff) and in others have apparently been destroyed (for example Abraham Bezalel).

In many cases, however, material regarding Russian political emigrants in Britain before 1917 is not in the archives of the emigrants themselves, but in the archives of those to whom they wrote or who wrote about them. One of the most interesting sources on A. I. Hertzen's stay in Britain in the 1850s and early 1860s, for instance, in his correspondence with Joseph Cowen, the Newcastle Radical MP and owner of the *Newcastle Chronicle*, which may be inspected in the Tyne & Wear Archives Department in Newcastle: this correspondence was used to effect by Professor Monica Partridge in her pioneering articles using British archival materials for the study of Russian history as early as the 1950s.

A fascinating sidelight on the character of P. A. Kropotkin is provided by his almost forty years' correspondence with John Scott Keltie,[25] a prominent member of the Royal Geographical Society and later editor of its *Geographical Magazine*. These letters are preserved in the Society's archives, and show the warm, humane side of a man who captivated British public opinion in spite of his apparently uncongenial political views (one recalls Oscar Wilde's characterization of him as a 'white Christ'): the letters show too his continuing interest in geographical theory and in Siberia, which both ran alongside and contributed to his political views for decades.

A similar unfamiliar insight into Stepniak's early activities in Britain—a period not covered by any other source than his own archive in the Central State Archive for Literature and Art (Tsentral'nyi gosudarstvennyi arkhiv literatury i iskusstva SSSR, TsGALI)—lies in the Karl Pearson Papers at University College, London, which contains letters to Pearson from Mrs Charlotte Wilson, the bluestocking wife of an indulgent City stockbroker and later founder-member of Kropotkin's 'Freedom' Group, and from Stepniak himself, dating from 1885 and early 1886, including a twelve-page explanation from Stepniak of the political views of the Russian 'nihilists', as Russian socialists of all stripes were then inevitably known in Britain. Mrs Wilson was trying to convert Pearson to the cause of Russian freedom—that is, anti-Tsarism—and Stepniak, to explain to him its political implications. All this activity came to nothing, however, for the Society of Friends of Russia which Mrs Wilson and Mrs Besant had dreamt up, and which Stepniak fell in with, was not to exist longer than six months.[26] But for this archival source, we would know nothing of it beyond a single paragraph in a radical newspaper.

Relating to the later, more frequently described, period of Stepniak's British exile are letters in English from him, Volkhovskii, Kropotkin and British members of the Society of Friends of Russian Freedom (SFRF) (1890–1914) contained in the Weiss Papers,[27] soon to be deposited in Newcastle University Library. These are letters addressed to and collected by members of the Spence Watson family, and contain a part of the papers of Robert Spence Watson (a Newcastle solicitor and at one time president of the National Liberal Federation): the other part was deposited in the House of Lords Records Office, but contains little of Russian interest. The Weiss Papers are, however, an essential source for the foundation and early history of the SFRF in the 1890s[28] as well as containing many other letters of great interest from other leading political figures of this time (G. B. Shaw and Edward Pease *inter alios*).

There are other letters in English from the trio of Stepniak, Volkhovskii and Kropotkin in many archives in Britain. They were all clearly assiduous correspondents. There is a large number in the British Library Additional Manuscripts collection, for instance, nearly all from the 1890s, again consisting of letters to G. B. Shaw and William Morris. The Hilton Hall Papers, consisting of papers of members of the Garnett family at present in the hospitable charge of Mr Richard Garnett at Hilton Hall, contain others. Part of Hilton Hall represents the papers of Constance Garnett, the pioneer translator of Russian literature, who was taught Russian by Feliks Volkhovskii,[29] and part is those of Olive Garnett, sister-in-law of Constance, minor novelist on Russian themes and friend of Stepniak.[30] There are letters to both ladies from Stepniak and Volkhovskii, dating from 1892–7, at Hilton Hall. Olive Garnett was deeply in love with Stepniak, although unrequitedly, as her diary reveals. This document, in private possession, is a most interesting source for Stepniak's life, albeit written from a hero-worshipping viewpoint, in the years 1893–5, when he was acting as Olive Garnett's literary adviser in her first efforts at writing, and she was his linguistic proof-reader. Olive Garnett's visit to Russia in 1896, like that of Constance Garnett four years earlier, was made at the suggestion of Stepniak and in pursuance of his political aims. Professor Tom Moser, the expert on Ford Madox Ford, has produced a so far unpublished paper based on Olive Garnett's diary and dealing with her unfulfilled relationship with Stepniak. Further letters from Constance Garnett to Feliks Volkhovskii, dating from 1892–8, a remainder from the Volkhovskii papers described earlier, are in private hands in Britain.[31] There is further Volkhovskii material, consisting of books, periodicals, proofs and drafts of minor material, in the Durham University Russian Research Collections, together with the Jaakoff Prelooker Collection, reflecting the life in Britain of the editor and publisher of *The Anglo-Russian* (1860–1935), and the Barry Hollingsworth archive, being the working papers of a pioneer scholar of the Russian emigration in British archives.[32].

Isolated letters from the various emigrants, especially those around the SFRF, are to be found in many archives throughout Britain: the Guy Aldred Papers in Glasgow's Baillie's Library, with yet more letters from Kropotkin; the archive of the Fabian Society (of which Stepniak was a member in the 1890s) at Nuffield College, Oxford; the Edward Carpenter Collection in Sheffield Public Library, with more Kropotkin letters as well as letters from Carpenter's Russian readers; Bromley Public Library, with Kropotkin letters; the National

Library of Scotland, with letters from Kropotkin to 'Don Roberto', the traveller and Scottish radical MP Robert Cunningham-Graham; letters from Kropotkin in the possession of Miss Daphne Sanger; letters from the Russian writer A. I. Ertel' to his daughter, the translator Nathalie Duddington, and from Russians in Britain to her;[33] minutes and letters in the archive of the Board of Deputies of British Jews (generally reflecting the condescension of Anglo-Jewry to their slightly embarrassing East European immigrant co-religionists); and numerous others.

Perhaps the largest of these random finds in collections devoted to other subjects is to be found in the British Library of Political and Economic Science. There, as well as the W. M. Voynich Collection (containing only a little material from his period of close contact with the Russian emigrants in the early 1890s) and the S. P. Mel'gunov Papers (with numerous copies of V. L. Burtsev's correspondence with various Russian revolutionaries between 1907 and 1913, among these G. V. Plekhanov, G. Lopatin, N. V. Chaikovskii *et al.*), the British Library of Political and Economic Science contains single letters from the SFRF group in the Lansbury, Solly and Courtney Collections, and additionally the Miscellaneous Collection (Volkhovskii and Kropotkin letters acquired, presumably, by purchase).

There undoubtedly remain other collections of archive material in Britain still to be discovered which will reflect new light on Russian politicals here before 1917: the increasing rate of discovery in recent years probably reflects an increase in the importance attached by historians to manuscript sources for the study of modern history. We seem to have lost for good the papers of Volkhovskii's English assistant, J. Frederick Green, and of Chicherin's parliamentary representative, Joseph King. On the Russian side, the archive of I. V. Shklovskii ('Dioneo'), for many years before the revolution English correspondent of a number of Russian newspapers and journals, who remained here in emigration after 1917 and died in the course of the last war, would be a tremendous find too.

Before worrying too much about these probable losses, however important, we should reckon up instead what remains extant and what probably still remains to be uncovered. It is for both these reasons, and not just for the first one, that Dr Hartley's survey is so welcome: not merely as a catalogue of what is, but as a means for arousing interest and rescuing what remains to be preserved.

Notes

1. P. M. Kerzhentsev, *Stolitsa Anglii* (Moscow, 1919), p. 89.
2. A survey of 1916 found over 30,000 conscriptable Russian males in Britain, mainly in London (Public Record Office, Home Office, HO45 10818/318095/—material from the public records is quoted with the permission of their Keeper). On the immigration policies which made this possible, see Bernard Porter, 'The British Government and the Political Refugees, 1880–1917' in *From the Other Shore: Russian political emigrants in Britain 1880–1917*, edited by John Slatter (London, 1984), pp. 23–48 (hereafter *FTOS*).
3. See Barry Hollingsworth, 'The Society of Friends of Russian Freedom: English Liberals and Russian Socialists, 1890–1917', *Oxford Slavonic Papers*, New Series 3 (1970), 45–64; and Ron Grant, 'The Society of Friends of Russian Freedom, 1890–1914: a Case Study in Internationalism', *Journal of the Scottish Labour History*, 3 (November 1970), 3–24.
4. See Alexander Brandenburg, 'Der kommunistische Arbeiterbildungsverein in London', *International Review of Social History* 24, no. 3 (1979), 341–70.
5. David Saunders, 'Vladimir Burtsev and the Russian Revolutionary Emigration (1888–1905)', *European Studies Review* 13, no. 1 (1983), 39–62.
6. Among a small number of items of Russian interest which the Library still possesses is a Russian typescript by Maksim Gor'kii describing his impressions of London during a visit here to the 1907 Social Democratic Party Congress.
7. T. Ossorguine, *L'Emigration russe en Europe: catalogue collectif des périodiques russes 1855–1940* (Paris, 1976), pp. 27–100.
8. The principal catalogues are V. M. Anderson, *Vol'naya russkaya pechat'*, (Peterburg [*sic*], 1922); Kenneth E.

Carpenter, *Russian Revolutionary Literature* (New Haven, 1976); A. A. Shilov, *Chto chitat' po istorii russkogo revolyutsionnogo dvizheniya* (Peterburg [*sic*], 1922); and E. Zaleski, *Mouvements ouvriers et socialistes: La Russie*, 2 vols (Paris, 1956).

9. Personal communication to the present author by Dr N. E. Andreev of 1 May 1981. Dr Andreev was in Prague in the 1930s and early to middle 1940s, and met Professor Sidorov again at a conference in Stockholm in later years.

10. Letters from his widow Cicely in the Soskice Papers make this clear: see *infra*, note 15.

11. But *N. V. Chaikovskii*, edited by A. A. Titov, 2 vols (Paris, 1929), is based on the Chaikovskii archive, though without references to specific parts of it.

12. See the Passfield Papers in the British Library of Political and Economic Science, and the Shaw Papers in British Library Additional Manuscripts, for correspondence about this sale. The Stepniak archive is now in TsGALI; see M. E. Ermasheva, *V londonskoi emigratsii* (Moscow, 1968), for excerpts from it. The call number in TsGALI is *fond* 1158, *edinitsa khraneniya* 871: for a short description of its contents see *Tsentral'nyi gosudartsvennyi arkhiv literatury i iskusstva SSSR: Putevoditel'*, vol. 2 (Moscow, 1963), p. 439.

13. *Lavrov: Years of Emigration*, edited by Boris Sapir, 2 vols (Dordrecht, 1974), publishes part of them.

14. Rocker's own autobiography, partly translated as *The London Years* (London, 1956), deals with his years of emigration here: William Fishman, *East End Jewish Radicals* (London, 1975) uses the archive.

15. Barry Hollingsworth, 'David Soskice in Russia in 1917', *European Studies Review*, 6, no. 1 (1976), 73–97, is based on a preliminary survey of the Soskice Papers, interrupted by Dr Hollingsworth's untimely and much regretted death. Caroline Rawcliffe, *The Stow Hill Papers* (London, 1977) and John Slatter, 'The Soskice Papers: A Guide', *Sbornik of the Study Group of the Russian Revolution*, 8 (1982), 47–68, form together a guide to the whole collection, which is kept in the House of Lords Record Office.

16. Ron Grant, 'G. V. Chicherin and the Russian Revolutionary

Cause in Britain', *FTOS*, pp. 117–40, is based on the Bridges Adams Papers, as Chicherin's First World War archive is known. The Papers are at present in the keeping of Dr Harry Shukman of St Antony's College, Oxford.

17. Part of which has been published, with a commentary derived from Soskice's own notes, in *Literaturnoe nasledie G. V. Plekhanova*, IV (Moscow, 1937), 301–6, V (1938), 299–301, and *Filosofsko–literaturnoe nasledie G. V. Plekhanova*, I (Moscow, 1973), 171; II (Moscow, 1973), 303.

18. Handlist 51 of the Brotherton Library, University of Leeds.

19. On life in Tuckton House in the early 1900s, see V. D. Bonch-Bruevich, *Izbrannye proizvedeniya*, II (Moscow, 1961), pp. 190–236.

20. On Mrs Bridges Adams, see the biography in *Dictionary of Labour Biography*, VI, edited by J. Saville and J. Bellamy (London, 1982), pp. 1–7.

21. Envelopes nos 3 and 6; boxes nos 5, 8, 14, 15.

22. On this episode, see Murdock Rodgers, 'The Anglo-Russian Military Convention and the Lithuanian Immigrant Community in Lanarkshire, Scotland, 1914–1920', *Immigrants and Minorities*, 1, no. 1 (March 1982), 60–88; R. K. Debo, 'The Making of a Bolshevik: Georgii Chicherin in England, 1914–1918', *Slavic Review*, 25 (1966), 551–62; Julia Bush, 'East London Jews and the First World War', *The London Journal*, 6, no. 2 (1980), 147–61; and Ron Grant, 'G. V. Chicherin'.

23. Colin Holmes, 'Government Files and Privileged Access', *Social History*, 6, no. 3 (October 1981), p. 343.

24. Among them, 'Alexander Herzen and the Younger Joseph Cowen, M.P.: some unpublished materials', *Slavonic and East European Review*, 41 (1962), 50–63; and 'Herzen, Ogaryov and the Free Russian Press in London', *Anglo-Soviet Journal*, 27, no. 1 (1966), 8–13.

25. See John Slatter, 'The Kropotkin Papers', *Geographical Magazine* (November 1981), 117–22.

26. John Slatter, 'Stepniak and the Friends of Russia', *Immigrants and Minorities*, 2, no. 1 (March 1983), 33–49.

27. Both John Slatter, 'Stepniak', and David Saunders, 'Stepniak and the London Emigration: Letters to Robert

Spence Watson (1887–1890)', *Oxford Slavonic Papers*, New Series 13 (1980), 80–93, have drawn on the Weiss Papers.

28. But see also, for other letters extracted from the Stepniak archive, M. E. Ermasheva, *op. cit.*

29. See David Garnett, *The Golden Echo* (London, 1953), chapters 1–5. Much of these chapters was taken from Constance's own autobiography, pencilled in an exercise-book, but unfinished, which is in the Hilton Hall Papers.

30. See her *St Petersburg Tales* (London, 1897) and *Night over Russia* (London, 1918).

31. I have used it in compiling *From the Other Shore*, a pamphlet designed to accompany an exhibition mounted in the University of Durham in 1981.

32. A catalogue is available on application to the Department of Russian, University of Durham. For some of Dr Hollingsworth's output, see notes 3 and 15 above.

33. See Sebastian Garrett, 'Unpublished Letters of the Russian Writer A. I. Ertel' to his daughter Nathalie Duddington' (unpublished M.Litt. thesis, University of Birmingham, 1983).

Revolution and Emigration: the Russian Files of the British and Foreign Bible Society, 1917–1970*

STEPHEN K. BATALDEN

Speaking recently on 'Problems of Biblical Translation', Czeslaw Milosz, Nobel poet laureate and translator of the Bible into modern Polish, pointed out how 'the appearance of literature in the vernacular in Europe is largely connected with translations and adaptations of the Bible'.[1] What his comment suggested as well, even though it has sometimes been forgotten, is that the documentary record of modern biblical translation and scholarship can serve to illumine issues of fundamental historical and cultural importance in a great many modern languages, not least the Russian. It is for just this reason that the library and archive of the British and Foreign Bible Society (BFBS) hold special value for historians and philologists.

Founded in 1804 by evangelical Christian leaders, the British and Foreign Bible Society gained the broad support of Anglicans

*I wish to express my appreciation to the archivist of the British and Foreign Bible Society, Ms Kathleen Cann, whose assistance has been particularly helpful in the preparation of this paper. In the last two decades Ms Cann has brought order and retrievability to a once unwieldy and uncatalogued collection. Her generous assistance to researchers is well-known to all who have used the collection.

On a related note, the library and archive of the Society has recently been moved to Cambridge, where the materials have been deposited on permanent loan as a separate collection within the Cambridge University Library. A small portion of the archive, primarily those records since the beginning of the Second World War, remains with the Bible Society which has moved its offices from London to Swindon. Archival materials at Cambridge have open access. Papers remaining in Swindon are available by special permission only.

and non-conformists alike in undertaking Bible translation, publication and distribution throughout much of Europe and the non-Western world. For Britain the BFBS became as much a social movement as an institution. Local affiliated branches, often including strong participation by women, swelled the Society's membership ranks as well as its treasury. In the first century of its existence, the BFBS sponsored publication of about 186,000,000 Bibles, in whole or in part, in 378 different languages.[2] By the turn of the century BFBS agents were located in over sixty countries.[3]

Prominent in this regard were the efforts of the BFBS within the Russian Empire. From 1812 until 1924 the BFBS had continuous representation in St Petersburg/Petrograd, expanding its operation in the nineteenth century to include formal agencies also in Odessa and Ekaterinburg (Sverdlovsk).[4] While the focus here is upon some of the lesser known twentieth-century Russian files of the BFBS, the most significant body of papers bearing on BFBS activity in Russia relates to the nineteenth century, the period of greatest translation and distribution activity. Voluminous foreign, home, and editorial correspondence, as well as formal committee and subcommittee minutes of the London offices, document in great detail the activity of BFBS agents in Russia.[5]

Leaving aside the central and much disputed issue of the translation of the modern Russian Bible, there are at least three other major issues for which the nineteenth-century papers have particular relevance. First, BFBS papers—especially the personal papers of John Paterson, Robert Pinkerton and Ebenezer Henderson—are critical for any study of the Imperial Russian Bible Society chartered by Alexander I at the end of 1812 and closed by imperial decree in 1826.[6] The BFBS played a seminal role in the founding and day to day operation of the Russian Bible Society. Although the full range of BFBS material has only been made accessible in the past two decades, the importance of the earlier collection for the history of the Russian Bible Society can be seen in the splendid Ph.D. dissertation on the topic written twenty years ago by Judith Cohen Zacek from BFBS papers.[7]

Second, the BFBS papers may be consulted to great advantage by scholars dealing with non-Russian nationalities of the

Empire. BFBS agents, particularly the Scot William Nicolson, oversaw and reported on Bible translation into several non-Russian languages of the Empire. The editorial correspondence of the BFBS is especially revealing in that regard, including records of biblical translations not only into Asian, particularly Turkic, languages of the Empire, but into Ukrainian, Baltic and Caucasian languages as well.[8] By 1913, BFBS depots in Russia were able to sell copies of the Bible in whole or in part in thirty-nine languages of the Empire—most of these translations having been commissioned at BFBS expense.[9] The records of these translation projects are of obvious value for the history of the Orthodox Missionary Society (*Pravoslavnoe missionerskoe obshchestvo*), with which organization BFBS agents co-operated. But these records also serve directly to document the role of biblical translation in the cultivation and preservation of numerous national languages of the Empire.

Finally, BFBS nineteenth-century records can be consulted to great advantage for the study of the growth of sectarianism or Protestantism in the last fifty years of the Empire. While there are other British collections which document ties with Protestants of the Russian Empire—Lieven, Pashkov and Radstock papers, for example—the study of Russian sectarianism still awaits the analysis of the colportage network generated by BFBS Russian agencies for the dissemination of biblical literature. That colportage effort, which was yielding distribution for BFBS Russian agencies of over 714,000 volumes annually by 1913, can be reconstructed, including the names of most colporteurs, from BFBS published records, as well as from correspondence and account books.[10] The relationship between scripture dissemination, movements for mass literacy, and the growth of Protestant subcultures in the Ukraine and elsewhere ought to be able to be clarified through use of these important records.

For all these matters there are now an impressive number of unpublished BFBS indexes to guide the user. The foreign, home and editorial correspondence of the BFBS is indexed annually, as are the committee and sub-committee minute books. For Russia, separately bound agents' copybooks have survived only for the years 1869 to 1874.[11] Finally, under the direction of the archivist, Ms Cann, an extensive biographical card file has been developed for foreign, home and editorial correspondence, thus providing an important short cut supplementing the handwritten annual indexes.[12]

For twentieth-century, post-First World War, developments, BFBS Russian papers are far less extensive, but no less interesting.[13] The impact of the Russian Revolution and the influence of Russian émigré leaders upon the BFBS can be seen in the three major issues that dominate the papers from 1917 to 1970. These issues are, in order of their appearance in the papers: (1) the closure and restructuring of BFBS Russian operations following the October 1917 Revolution; (2) the conflict in the 1920s with Soviet evangelicals over the funding of Bible publication in the Soviet Union; and (3) after a hiatus in BFBS Russian activity from the late 1920s until after the Second World War, BFBS sponsorship of a new Russian translation of the New Testament.

The Bolshevik Revolution, the ensuing civil war, and the nationalization of privately-owned property ultimately combined to undermine BFBS agency operations in Russia, but in the short term BFBS agencies continued to function with limited success, lasting in Petrograd until the very end of 1924. The Siberian agency at Ekaterinburg was the first to close its operation, falling victim to the turbulent civil war. Walter Davidson, the permanent British agent for the BFBS in Ekaterinburg since that agency's founding in 1889, left Ekaterinburg with his wife in the spring of 1918. Abandoning investments in Russian property and stock, they escaped the civil war by fleeing through Siberia to Japan, and then returned to England.[14] The BFBS Siberian agency was left in charge of Davidson's assistant, Kvadratus Ivanovich Bjelousoff (i.e. Belousov). Belousov sought to keep the agency operating into 1919, but, even after the temporary liberation of Ekaterinburg from Soviet control in July 1918, the lack of an available fresh supply of scriptures from Petrograd and the subsequent rounds of civil war activity rendered the BFBS Ekaterinburg agency and its colportage activity inactive by the end of 1919.[15]

The Petrograd agency managed to survive longer than the Siberian agency. In the autumn of 1917, William Kean, the British agent of the Bible Society in Petrograd, successfully negotiated with the Holy Synod a printing of the Russian Bible without the apocrypha—the apocryphal or non-canonical Old Testament books having been a matter of contention between BFBS and Synodal interests since the publication of their rival Old Testaments in the 1870s.[16] Along with overseeing colportage and other depot accounts in Petrograd, Kean saw this Synodal/Patriarchal printing through the press for the BFBS in early 1918.

Still, all was not routine. In March 1918, Kean reported to London that, despite the availability of scriptures in Petrograd, communication had by then been broken with four of the BFBS sub-depots—those in Odessa, Tiflis, Tashkent and Helsinki.[17] As the foreign community became ever smaller in Petrograd by late 1918, Kean moved his own residence into the British-American Congregational Church, there acting as secretary to the British Relief Committee.[18] In December 1918, word reached the BFBS in London that its agent William Kean had died of a cerebral haemorrhage caused by an accidental fall down a staircase.[19]

The death of William Kean, the last British agent of the BFBS in Russia, forced the Society to reconsider the nature of its operations in revolutionary Russia. For the short term, the Society was content to have its Petrograd depot run by Kean's former assistants, the Latvian evangelical Andrei Gustavovich Neiman and, later, the Russian Orthodox colporteur Evtikhii Petrovich Maslennikov. As the widowed Mrs Kean noted before leaving Petrograd in the spring of 1919, 'Neyman still keeps the Petrograd Depot open and up to now the proceeds of the sales have covered the expenses, Neyman's salary included, and left a small margin'.[20] As it turned out, Kean had given instructions before his death that all other BFBS depots were to be closed and existing furniture and stock were to be sold. From the perspective of the London central offices, what that meant was that an operation which only five years prior had been distributing over 700,000 volumes annually in the Russian Empire through an elaborate system of sub-depots and colporteurs now was to have a lone holding operation in Petrograd supervised by a former depot assistant and one colporteur.

While the loss to its mission was obvious, the actual financial losses incurred by the Society were less serious.[21] Alongside the great losses sustained by such British commercial interests as the Moscow department store of Muir and Mirrielees Ltd, the

Society's assets, mostly in stock inventory, were not a major consideration.[22] Neiman and Maslennikov were to continue selling off the BFBS stock even after all bookstores were nationalized in May 1920. Finally, in December 1924, the last stock was sold on commission to Ivan Stepanovich Prokhanov and his All-Union Council of Evangelical Christians. At the same time, the remains of William Kean's substantial library and the papers of the BFBS Petersburg agency were handed over for temporary deposit to Prokhanov's All-Union Council.[23] Neiman and Maslennikov, along with other career colporteurs and BFBS depot employees in the Soviet Union, continued to receive pensions until their death or until all communication was broken in the 1930s.

While London BFBS offices helped to finance the single Petrograd outpost until 1924, they also laid plans for re-entry into Russia when, as they assumed would be the case, the time would soon be more favourable. Within four months of the news of Kean's death the Society was recommending that Walter Davidson, the former Ekaterinburg agent, be put at the head of a combined Russian and Siberian agency.[24] Apparently thought was initially given to sending Davidson back to Vladivostok where his assistant Belousov was holding out for, when a year later the action was taken to send Davidson, a BFBS secretary noted the matter of 'Mr. Davidson's return not to Vladivostok but to Finland'.[25] Davidson left for Helsinki in the spring of 1920 to establish a BFBS North-East European Agency. The reasons for sending the veteran Russian expert to that agency were those of preparation for re-entry into Russia 'at the first moment' and maintenance of ties with the Petrograd depot. From 1920, Helsinki became the new focal point for BFBS Russian initiatives. Under the leadership of Walter Davidson (1920–5), W. J. Wiseman (1925–37), and the depositary G. G. Pimenoff (1927–55), the Helsinki North-East European Agency of the BFBS brought continuity of personnel to a Russian field in which political discontinuities severely restricted BFBS action inside the Soviet Union.[26]

The papers of the new BFBS North-East European Agency are dominated by one central Russian issue of the 1920s—namely, the turbulent relationship between the BFBS and Soviet sectarian, evangelical leaders. Who were these Russian sectarians?

Protestant movements in Russia and the Soviet Union have of late received increasing attention from historians. In addition to the memoirs of major participants, there have now been studies on both the evolving All-Russian Union of Baptists and I. S. Prokhanov's All-Russian Union of Evangelical Christians (this latter group being the one whose Council received the Kean library and BFBS Petersburg papers).[27]

Although their numbers grew substantially from the 1870s under the influence of the Pashkovite and Radstock urban meetings and the spread of Bible reading and prayer groups in the Ukraine, Protestants in the Russian Empire, including the once-privileged German groups of the south, remained subject to state restrictions against proselytizing. Until the 1905 Revolution and the dismantling of Konstantin Pobedonostsev's machinery directed against sectarians and Old Believers, Protestant believers were subjected to occasional persecution and harassment. Despite the recurrence of some of these anti-sectarian measures after 1906, the pre-war years saw the continued growth and development of Protestantism in Russia. Several Russian Protestants, notably the young Ivan Prokhanov, studied in British or other Western seminaries or Bible schools, and Russian Protestant publications, including a famous collection of Russian hymns, the *Gusli* (the harp, or psaltery), gained wide circulation within the Empire.[28] It was, however, following the October Bolshevik Revolution that the sectarian movement entered upon its period of greatest expansion, a period which continued well into the 1920s.

It was at this critical moment in the history of Russian evangelicalism that the BFBS entered into sustained correspondence and maintained personal links with the two most important Soviet Protestant leaders of the 1920s—Ivan S. Prokhanov of the All-Russian Union of Evangelical Christians and Pavel V. Pavlov of the All-Russian Union of Baptists.[29] Prokhanov and Pavlov, who became bitter rivals in the world of Soviet sectarian politics, shared a measure of immunity from state restrictions, travelling to the West on several occasions in the 1920s. The rather favourable attitude of the new Soviet government, especially in the person of Vladimir Bonch-Bruevich, Lenin's personal secretary and an authority on *sektantsvo* and *staroobryadchestvo* (sectarianism and Old Belief),

provided considerable latitude for these groups. Whether the
new order viewed them as fellow-opponents of the old regime or
simply an additional divisive force directed against the Russian
Orthodox patriarchal leadership, the Protestants used this opening to great advantage. Energetic leaders such as Prokhanov and
Pavlov directed famine relief work, church publication efforts,
seminary instruction, urban ministry, and effective revivalist
preaching. Thousands attended Protestant services in Moscow
and Leningrad throughout the 1920s.

The papers of the BFBS do not address this rather spectacular
success story of Russian Protestantism, but rather reveal a quite
different picture of Soviet Protestant leaders as they turned
to the West in dramatic fund-raising appeals. The finances of
Soviet Protestantism have always been a rather murky, sub-
terranean issue, and the BFBS records reveal the frustration of
Bible Society and Western church leaders as they sought to deal
with these very effective, if highly manipulative, Soviet fund-
raisers.[30] In the case of the BFBS, and also the American Bible
Society, Prokhanov and Pavlov sought to gain the financial support of these agencies for a large scripture publication programme
in the USSR.[31] The two rival leaders also sought to have transferred to their respective organizations Russian scriptures held
by BFBS repositories whether in the Soviet Union or abroad.

Given the nature of the BFBS as primarily a publishing concern and not a religious or denominational body, the BFBS
Helsinki agent Walter Davidson and the London secretaries
became more than a little agitated over the unwillingness of the
Soviet Protestant leaders to reveal the record of their sales, to say
nothing of the margin of their profits.[32] Already by 1922,
Walter Davidson wrote back to London with the following
admonition:

> I am under the impression that Mr. Prochanoff is out to
> secure the sole monopoly for selling the Scriptures in Russia.
> I have collected quite a mine of information about this good
> man, and the work he is carrying on in Russia. ... My
> common sense tells me that he is a powerful factor in the
> shaping of the new Evangelical bodies in Russia, and will have
> a good deal to do in carrying out a defined policy towards the
> old Greek Orthodox Church. Many of his followers are

simply too lopsided in their views on this important subject to merit serious attention by thoughtful Christians. We, as a Bible Society, must avoid linking ourselves up with any such organization. I am on good terms with them all, and strive to give offence to none. ... Believing this, and firmly convinced that it is the only position we can take up in Russia, I am against giving any special terms to any of these bodies, and more especially to that of Mr. Prochanoff.[33]

In the same letter, Davidson alluded to the support being provided by Dr Rushbrooke, the Baptist Commissioner for Europe:

I note that Dr. Rushbrooke has paid in a sum of money (£14,000) towards the cost of the edition of the Bible in Russ at present being printed in Germany. The Baptists have the money, and the brethren in Russia know it.[34]

By 1925, after three years of correspondence and meetings had passed between Walter Davidson and Prokhanov and Pavlov, the Helsinki BFBS agent Davidson summed up his reactions in a letter to London. He wrote:

At present there is sort of scramble, or race, to capture the monopoly of printing the Scriptures in Russia. ... Mr. Prokhanoff is still here and remains for another week; Pavlov ought to be back from Stockholm in three–four days. Both of these men are, I am sure, keeping in touch with the Soviet [authorities] and, to a certain extent (perhaps unwittingly), doing the present Government in Russia favours. They are making appeals for money to assist them in carrying on their work and both are looking to their brethren in the U.S., and even trying to raise the wind to get across there themselves.

They naturally won't show their hands to me, but I firmly believe that one strong plank in their appeal is the 'want of the Scriptures'.

Now P[rokhanov] is preparing an appeal and in this document he sets forth the liberty, the contrast between the old days and now, for evangelising Russia! The taint of propaganda runs right through it, every statement, even the figures, every inference is subject to this discount. P[rokhanov] wants to bring out the best points of the present regime. Pavloff is on the same footing; both men do not seem to notice the strong leaning towards this Bolshevism, they have become accustomed to the atmosphere, the environment, and it sickens me. ... I am aware of the persecutions of former days, the horrors of what the clergy and others went through in 1918–1919 and my heart, I hope, is not hardened, or my charity lessened, but I do think that we cannot budge one inch from the present standpoint, i.e., *to give them no more books on credit.*[35]

Davidson's concerns do not challenge the claim that Russian sectarianism was thriving in the Soviet Union in the 1920s. Instead, the archive of the British and Foreign Bible Society documents another side, albeit a rather seamy fund-raising side, of that movement. It is a record worthy of examination. Prokhanov, for his part, left the Soviet Union for good in 1928, continuing his appeals for the All-Russian Union of Evangelical Christians in the United States and Western Europe until his death in 1935. Soviet evangelical leaders in the 1920s were complicated, gifted religious figures during a period when Bonch-Bruevich and others were prepared to give them some latitude for their machinations. That period of grace ended by 1928–9, and with it also all significant ties between the BFBS and Soviet churches.

Despite the breakdown in communication with the Soviet Union and with Soviet Protestant leaders, Bible Society interest in the Russian Bible continued. In particular, the BFBS was concerned that, if there were to be some official opening for the Society in Russia, it should have an adequate text ready in an appropriate orthography. Alongside the Helsinki operations, London offices consulted Sir Bernard Pares who, in 1937, suggested the Society establish ties with St Sergius Theological Institute in Paris.[36] Later, Professor Pares was to serve on the Society's governing board, the General Committee.

Even before the Second World War drew to a close, BFBS Russian relations entered a new phase, one marked by significant overtures to Russian Orthodox émigré circles. This new development began in late 1941 in conversations between Nicholas Zernov, a prominent figure in émigré circles, and the Society's 'postwar planning subcommittee'.[37] From Zernov the ties led to George Fedotov in the United States, and from the United States back to St Sergius Theological Institute in Paris. What ultimately grew out of these BFBS explorations was the Society's commitment to sponsor a major new Russian translation of the New Testament, only the second to be undertaken since the reign of Alexander II (the other being that of Konstantin Pobedonostsev, St Petersburg, 1906).

BFBS records suggest that at the outset the Society was cautious about entering into such a far-reaching project. An initial proposal made in 1946–7 by an émigré acquaintance of Zernov, Yury D. Bezsonov, never secured the Society's support.[38] While the Society expressed concern for a good Russian text closer to the common language, what it was primarily concerned about initially was that any new translation have the political backing of all the Russian church jurisdictions.[39] Paul B. Anderson, a prominent American Russianist attached to the Paris YMCA, was to provide an important linkage between the Society and the Paris Russian religious intelligentsia. Anderson inquired of Father Georges Florovsky and representatives of the Paris Institute, reporting back to the American Bible Society General Secretary Eric North in the spring of 1950, that 'they all quite agree that a new translation is desirable'.[40]

Faced with mounting American Bible Society interest in such a project, the BFBS Translations Subcommittee decided to send its translations secretary, Wilford J. Bradnock, to Paris to meet all the interested parties. Those meetings, held in September 1950, were decisive. Bradnock returned to London fully prepared to underwrite the project, despite the fact that the Moscow Patriarch's representative, Archimandrite Yeremin, had already withdrawn from the project on instructions from Moscow. Moreover, it was at Bradnock's own suggestion that the project was broadened to constitute a completely new translation, not a mere 'Russification' removing archaisms in the 1862 Synodal New Testament translation.[41]

During Bradnock's Paris visit he had met a committee from the St Sergius Institute headed by the Rector and Professor of New Testament studies, Bishop Cassian (i.e., Kassian, Sergei Sergeevich Bezobrazov, 1892–1965). From that meeting it was clear to Bradnock that there was suitable expertise to undertake the project. Bishop Cassian would be the chief translator from the Greek, and a committee composed of as wide a jurisdictional cross-section as possible would review and revise Cassian's Russian text. Work would begin with the Gospel of Matthew, and it was hoped that a New Testament text would be completed within two or three years. The BFBS agreed to pay Bishop Cassian's salary for two and a half years of released time, and they allotted substantial support for secretarial services and travel costs of the committee members as well as of Bishop Cassian.[42] Donald Lowrie, the replacement for Paul Anderson at the Paris YMCA, would attend and minute sessions of the revision committee as a local representative for the BFBS.

There were several quite extraordinary elements in this BFBS project and, by way of summary, it is well to note the participants, language, textology and actual production of what has come to be called the 'Cassian New Testament'. Despite the official withdrawal of the Moscow Patriarchate from the project and the general lack of interest shown on the part of the Munich-based church-in-exile, there was initially broad interest in the project. Committee membership read like a 'who's who' of first-wave Russian émigré religious leaders. The special ties of the Constantinople Ecumenical Patriarch Athenagoras to the St Sergius Institute and to Bishop Cassian personally were evidenced in a letter of blessing which he sent to the project.[43] Many other clerical and lay leaders attached themselves to the project as corresponding members. The inner revision committee came to include, at one time or another, the following notable scholars: Wladimir W. Weidle, N. A. Koulomzin, Boris K. Zaitzeff, Vladimir N. Lossky, Vladimir N. Rayevsky, Anton V. Kartasheff, John Meyendorff, Dimitri Obolensky, Alexei Kniazeff, Ilia Melia, A. P. Wassilieff and, of course, Bishop Cassian.[44]

Predictably, all was not harmonious. When word reached Russian evangelical circles of the new translation project, appeals came in to the BFBS for adequate representation. Pastor A. P. Wassilieff, a leading Russian Protestant and Bible school superintendent in Brussels, was quickly added to the committee.[45] A much greater crisis, which threatened to abort the whole project, was the conflict over capitalization of pronominal references to Mary, the mother of Jesus. Ultimately the BFBS was obliged to issue two different variants of a 'trial edition' (*probnyi vypusk*) of the Gospel of Matthew with one coloured cover for the variant excluding capitalization, a different coloured cover for the variant including pronominal capitalization.[46] That edition of the Gospel of Matthew came to be called in London the 'tentative Matthew'.

In the long run what was most serious and what undermined BFBS interests in an easily readable text was the determination of Bishop Cassian to follow an almost literal translation of the Greek text. Cassian's slavish commitment to the Greek, perhaps reinforced by his own residence on Mount Athos during the Second World War, occasionally seemed almost Byzantine, as was his belief, only occasionally followed, that it was possible to replicate the original word order in the Russian rendering of the Gospel of John.[47] In the final analysis, no one on the revision committee was fully able to counteract this Russian linguistic usage problem. BFBS Translations Secretary Bradnock, who deferred to Lowrie and his successor Robbins Strong in the meeting-to-meeting details, did not know Russian. Here there was a notable difference between BFBS post-Second World War expertise and that of earlier periods when the Society had Russian agents such as Nicolson, Kean and Davidson who could command the language. Even though Bradnock quickly grasped the nature of the problem and sought to give greater authority to an internal literary panel led by Boris Zaitzeff and Wladimir Weidle, Bishop Cassian's archaic use of Russian was never entirely overcome. It proved to be the single greatest liability of the text.

In contrast to the linguistic problem, the textology of the Cassian New Testament proved to be its greatest contribution and served as a powerful stimulant to New Testament textual study in the Soviet Union. Bishop Cassian was fully conversant with Greek textological scholarship and used as the basis for his translation a revised critical Greek text of Eberhard Nestle.[48] The Synodal New Testament, on the contrary, had been based on an adapted Erasmian Greek New Testament, the co-called *textus receptus*. Beginning in 1954, faculty of the Moscow and Leningrad Theological Academies wrote extended articles in the *Zhurnal Moskovskoi Patriyarkhii* (Journal of the Moscow Patriarchate) reviewing the 'tentative Matthew' and defending the nineteenth-century Synodal translation and its use of the *textus receptus*.[49] As if to give greater force to its position, the Moscow

Patriarchate issued a new printing of the Synodal Bible in 1956, one of the relatively few reprintings in the Soviet period.[50]

In July 1955, a delegation of visiting Soviet churchmen was fêted at the BFBS London offices, at which time Bradnock gave the Leningrad Academy Rector (the young Bishop Nikodim) and the Archbishop of Minsk copies of Cassian's notes which offered Greek textual justifications for changes in the Synodal text.[51] Later, in 1960, in response to growing Soviet interest, a more complete set of Cassian's notes was prepared in a microfilm edition which Bishop Nikodim took back by hand to the USSR from his visit to Paris.[52] It is worth noting that the same Bishop Nikodim, as Metropolitan of Leningrad, launched later in the 1960s a Russian Biblical Commission at the Leningrad Theological Academy which, in 1975, became the 'Group for Biblical Research'.[53] In short, Bishop Cassian's abandonment of the Erasmian Greek *textus receptus* proved not only to be a watershed in Russian New Testament studies, but also spawned a lively and productive debate which still continues within Soviet theological circles.

Meanwhile, Bishop Cassian completed his translation, retiring for concentrated work to his seaside hideaway in Javea, Spain.[54] Following committee revision, the BFBS published the text in several instalments—the trial edition of Matthew (1953), an edition of the Gospels (1958), the Gospels with the Acts of the Apostles (1963), and the complete New Testament (1970). The rather hostile reception which the 'tentative Matthew' received tended to limit BFBS publishing interest. The result was that publication of the entire Russian New Testament did not follow until 1970, five years after Bishop Cassian's death.[55] In addition to marking the final posthumous publication of the Cassian New Testament, 1970 marked the year when all BFBS involvement in Russian matters was superseded by the international United Bible Societies, its European regional office. But it is the BFBS records, including both the microfilm of Bishop Cassian's notes and the exhaustively, almost verse by verse, minuted meetings of the revision committee that constitute fundamental documentary resources for future Russian New Testament studies in the Soviet Union and the West.

In 1941, following Russian entry into the war, Sir Bernard Pares wrote in the *Times Literary Supplement*:

Some of our closest and most inspiring contacts with Russia have been those of religion. Hardly any British institution has had a longer or better foothold there than the British and Foreign Bible Society, whose work particularly appealed to Alexander I after our joint victory over Napoleon. Its difficult task taught it great tact and wisdom. It does not force its services; it confines itself to circulating the Bible among those who will take it, and that is the only way that promises any success. ... The Bible Society is as active as ever.[56]

Pares's sympathetic remarks are now a bit dated. The British and Foreign Bible Society no longer has a role in the Soviet Union, and it is still too early to determine whether the United Bible Societies can be as resourceful as their British parent. But the archives of the Bible Society remain a valuable legacy for students of Russian culture and British-Russian relations.

Notes

1. Czeslaw Milosz, 'Problems of Biblical Translation', a lecture delivered at Arizona State University, 20 January 1984.
2. *Hundredth Report of the British and Foreign Bible Society* (London, 1904), p. 451 and appendix p. 25. This annual numbered *Report of the British and Foreign Bible Society* is the most important published guide to the activities of the Society. See also the following histories of the Society: John Owen, *The History of the Origin and First Ten Years of the British and Foreign Bible Society*, 2 vols (London, 1816), with a supplementary third volume covering the years 1814–19 (London, 1820); George Browne, *The History of the British and Foreign Bible Society from Its Institution in 1804 to the Close of Its Jubilee in 1854* (London, 1859); William Canton, *A History of the British and Foreign Bible Society*, 5 vols (London, 1904–10); and James Moulton Roe, *A History of the British and Foreign Bible Society, 1905–1954* (London, 1965).
3. 'List of Foreign Depots', in *Hundredth Report*, appendix pp. (1–10).

4. Archival records of the BFBS document the activities of the following British agency representatives in Russia (asterisks denote full-time BFBS paid agents):

*John Paterson (St Petersburg), 1812–26
*Ebenezer Henderson (St Petersburg), 1816–25
*Robert Pinkerton (St Petersburg), 1814–23
 Richard Knill (St Petersburg), 1826–33
 John Brown (St Petersburg), 1833–40
 Thomas Ellerby (St Petersburg), 1840–53
 Archibald Mirrielees (St Petersburg), 1853–7
 William Mirrielees (St Petersburg), 1857–65
 Andrew Muir (St Petersburg), 1860–9
*Adalbert Eck (St Petersburg), 1865–9
*William Nicolson (St Petersburg), 1869–97
*William Kean (St Petersburg/Petrograd), 1896–1918
 John Melville (Odessa), 1839–67
*James Watt (Odessa), 1867–82
*Michael Morrison (Odessa), 1882–95
*Walter Davidson (Ekaterinburg), 1889–1918.

5. There is no published guide to the BFBS archive. The previous archivist, Ms Kathleen Cann, prepared a substantial unpublished working catalogue of holdings. Within that catalogue there is, for Russia, a brief résumé of the main categories of home and foreign correspondence, as well as committee minute books. See 'The British and Foreign Bible Society: Part II, The Records (2 pp.)', a typescript guide to BFBS holdings, 1983, pp. 1–5.

6. The papers of John Paterson are identified as follows: BFBS Deposited Papers, Paterson Papers: Memoirs (1805–1850) and Papers (1808–1847) of BFBS Agent John Paterson. A portion of these papers has been published in Paterson's *The Book for Every Land*, second edition (London, 1858).

7. Judith Cohen Zacek, 'The Russian Bible Society, 1812–1826' (unpublished Ph.D. dissertation, Columbia University, 1964).

8. BFBS Editorial Correspondence Inwards (1858–97, 35 vols), BFBS Editorial Correspondence Outwards (1832–1908), and BFBS Editorial Subcommittee Minutes (from

1830) document issues involving translation of the Bible into non-Russian languages of the Empire. An arbitrary sample of four of the many languages involved— Chuvash, Estonian, Georgian and Ukrainian—provides evidence, even on the surface, of how significant are the BFBS records.

In the case of the Turkic Chuvash language, BFBS papers document the translation of the Gospels done in Kazan' in 1820 by the Russian Bible Society. However, the basic revision of the Gospels, the completion of the New Testament text and the rendering of the Psalter and other Old Testament books date from the 1870s and the translation work of Ivan Yakovlevich Yakovlev (1848–1930). A student of the Kazan' Tatar specialist Nikolai Ivanovich Il'minskii, Yakovlev worked with the Orthodox Missionary Society and BFBS agent William Nicolson in the preparation of his Chuvash translations. Yakovlev became a distinguished professor at the Simbirsk (Ul'yanovsk) Chuvash Institute which today bears his name. See *I. Ya. Yakovlev i ego shkola*, edited by G. N. Volkov, in *Uchenye zapiski Chuvashskogo gos. pedagogicheskogo inst. imeni I.Ya. Yakovleva*, Vyp. 33 (Cheboksary, 1971). This book, the result of a special session honoring the 120th anniversary of Yakovlev's birth and the 100th anniversary of the Simbirsk school, includes publication of Yakovlev's November 1920 letter to Lenin in which Yakovlev notes his ties with Lenin's father. There is no mention in the book of Yakovlev's Chuvash Bible translations. Yakovlev's BFBS-sponsored Chuvash translations were published in Kazan' and Simbirsk from the 1890s. The BFBS Library contains a very rare incomplete copy of the Chuvash Pentateuch printed during the First World War, but left unbound in signatures. The signatures run to chapter nineteen of the Book of Numbers before publication was stopped in 1918. Continuing correspondence with Yakovlev on Chuvash translation may be found in BFBS Editorial Correspondence: Turkish Chuvash, 1909–25. Readers of Jaroslav Hašek's *Bulugma Stories* will recall with a smile how important it was to note during the Russian civil war the Christian sensitivities of the Chuvash.

In the case of Estonian, the base texts for both southern and northern dialects date to the end of the seventeenth and eighteenth centuries. In both cases, revisions were undertaken in the nineteenth century under the Russian Bible Society's support and, later, under American Bible Society and BFBS sponsorship. For the work of Meyer (Psalter, 1836), Kiel (New Testament and Psalter, 1857), Masing (New Testament and Psalter, 1900), and Malm (1896 Bible), BFBS records can be utilized. Continuing correspondence on recent Estonian translation work, including the 1968 London Bible revised by Koolmeister, Kopp, Aavik, Roos and Pold, may be found in BFBS Editorial Correspondence: Estonian, 1913–66, 3 files.

In the case of Georgian, the *editio princeps* of the Bible is the translation of Prince Vakhusht, published in Moscow in 1743. Orthographical and textual revisions, however, date from the time of the Russian Bible Society and then reflect continuing BFBS involvement. The Old Testament revision of 1884, Bishop Leonid's 1896 New Testament, Archimandrite Kesari's 1895 Psalter, and Archpriest Peter Konchoshvili's 1900 Pentateuch all are documented in BFBS editorial records. Continuing correspondence on Georgian translations may be found in BFBS Editorial Correspondence: Georgian, 1910–73, 2 files.

Because of the greater latitude accorded Ukrainian literary publication in the Austrian Empire, virtually all modern Ukrainian biblical translation projects before 1905 were sponsored by the BFBS Vienna agency. Even some texts with a L'vov/L'viv imprint were actually printed in Vienna. For the account of these translations, including the work of P. A. Kulish, A. Kobilyan'ski, I. Pulyui, A. Slusarchuk, and I. Levits'ki, see the BFBS Vienna agency copybooks and BFBS editorial correspondence from the 1870s. For continuing correspondence on Ukrainian translations, see BFBS Editorial Correspondence: Ukrainian, 1909–70, 7 files. These more recent files document, among other projects, the major BFBS translation project under the chief translatorship of Metropolitan Ivan Ilarion (Ohijenko). That project culminated in the publication of the 1962 London Ukrainian Bible.

9. For distribution according to language, see 'Supplementary Tables of Circulation, Etc.' in *Hundred and Tenth Report* ... (London, 1914), appendix pp. (11–12).
10. For distribution figures, see *Hundred and Tenth Report* (London, 1914), pp. 90, 105. An easy guide to colporteurs is also the annual published 'Statistical Summary and Details of Colportage' in the numbered reports. For 1913–14, there were 101 Russian colporteurs and hawkers identified by name and province in the annual report, ibid., appendix pp. 12–14.
11. BFBS Agents Books, Russia, 4 vols, 1869–74. These four volumes (nos 125, 137, 142, and 149) are part of a larger series, but pre-1869 and post-1874 volumes for Russia do not survive.
12. The biographical card file indexes BFBS Foreign Correspondence Inwards, 1804–56; BFBS Home Correspondence Inwards, 1804–36; BFBS Editorial Correspondence Inwards, 1858–97; BFBS Agents' Books, 1867–77; The Paterson Deposited Papers, 1807–47; and occasional miscellaneous correspondence inwards.
13. In addition to committee minutes, there are three basic categories of BFBS papers for the later period: (1) BFBS Secretaries' Correspondence (Sec. Cor.): Russia, 1919–27 (two files of miscellaneous letters); (2) BFBS Deposited Papers (Dep. Papers): The Wiseman Papers, 1919–29 (including correspondence of the secretaries for northeastern Europe, Walter Davidson and W. J. Wiseman); and (3) BFBS Editorial Correspondence (Ed. Cor.): Russian, 1909– (including incoming and outgoing letters on Russian and Belorussian translations).
14. BFBS Staff Registers: Walter Davidson, 27 March 1923, 4 pp.
15. BFBS Foreign Accounts: Siberia, copy of Bjelousoff—Davidson, Ekaterinburg, 11/24 January 1919. Belousov left Ekaterinburg at the end of 1919, and took up residence and colportage in Chita until December 1921. From Chita he moved to Vladivostok where he continued to sell Bibles until 1923. From mid–1923, Belousov took residence in Harbin, Manchuria, where he continued colportage for the BFBS among the Russian population throughout the inter-war period. See BFBS China Subcommittee Minutes, vol. 9, 22 October 1923, p. 282.

16. For the synodal printing, see BFBS Foreign Depots Sub-committe Minutes, vol. 19, 15 November 1917, p. 236.

17. BFBS Minutes of the General Committee, vol. 118, 19 August 1918, p. 345.

18. Ibid., 18 November 1918, p. 471.

19. Ibid., 16 December 1918, p. 499; and 3 February 1919, p. 577.

20. Ibid., vol. 119, 16 June 1919, pp. 155–6.

21. Copy of S. N. Rostron's receipt to Mrs Kean, 8 August 1919, BFBS Foreign Accounts: Russia, A/Cs from September 1917.

22. The Moscow store of Muir & Mirrielees, still known today by that name, but officially the *Tsentral'nyi Gosudarstvennyi Univermag* opposite the Bolshoi Theatre, was built by the heirs of Archibald Mirrielees and his brother-in-law Andrew Muir, both of whom played vital roles in the day to day direction of the BFBS in St Petersburg from the 1830s until the later 1860s. See note 4 above. Correspondence of Archibald Mirrielees, his son William Mirrielees, and Andrew Muir is well represented in the BFBS archive, particularly in BFBS Foreign Correspondence Inwards and BFBS Editorial Correspondence Inwards. For the history and fate of Muir & Mirrielees, Ltd, which had estimated capital assets of over £1,300,000 seized at the time of the Revolution, see the Public Record Office, Foreign Office, FO 371, vol. 4000, no. 208147 (1920), pp. 410–18.

23. E. P. Maslennikov to Walter Davidson, Petrograd, 2 April 1924, and Leningrad, 24 December 1924, in BFBS Deposited Papers, Wiseman Papers (North-East European Agency), file no. 12 (Maslennikov, 1919–24).

24. BFBS Foreign Depots Subcommittee Minutes, vol. 19, 17 April 1919, pp. 133–4.

25. 'Reconstruction in Russia and Siberia', extract of Foreign Depots Subcommittee Minutes, 11 March 1920, p. 5, in BFBS Sec. Cor.: Russia, File 1b.

26. BFBS Staff Register, Wilfrid James Wiseman, died 14 August 1970; and BFBS Staff Register, George G. Pimenoff, died 8 May 1955. One of the coincidental ties between the Helsinki agency and the Paris translation project noted

later in this paper is that which Pimenoff maintained with Orthodox circles at St Sergius Institute. Pimenoff indicated that 'Professor N. Berdyaev in Paris [was] the godfather of my boy' (G. G. Pimenoff to W. J. Wiseman, Helsinki, 5 May 1938, BFBS Dep. Papers: Wiseman Papers, Correspondence with G. G. Pimenoff).

27. Representative of the memoirs is that of I. S. Prokhanov, *In the Cauldron of Russia, 1869–1933: Autobiography of I. S. Prokhanoff, Founder and Honorary President of the All-Russian Evangelical Christian Union; The Life of an Optimist in the Land of Pessimism together with an Interesting History of the Russian Evangelical Christian Union* (New York, 1933). On Prokhanov's Union, see Wilhelm Kahle, *Evangelische Christen in Russland und der Sowjetunion: Ivan Stepanovich Prochanov (1869–1935) und der Weg der Evangeliums-christen und Baptisten* (Wuppertal, 1978). On the Baptists, see Paul D. Steeves, 'The Russian Baptist Union, 1917–1935: Evangelical Awakening in Russia' (unpublished Ph.D. thesis, University of Kansas, 1976). See also Andrew Blane, 'The Relations Between the Russian Protestant Sects and the State, 1900–1921' (unpublished dissertation, Duke University, 1964). For an account of recent developments, see Walter Sawatsky, *Soviet Evangelicals Since World War II* (Scottdale, Pennsylvania, 1981).

28. *Gusli: Sbornik dukhovnykh pesen s notami, sostavlen I. S. Prokhanovym* (St Petersburg, 1909).

29. BFBS records on this question may be found in the following collections: BFBS Sec. Cor.: Russia, 1919–27; and BFBS Dep. Papers, The Wiseman Papers.

30. Prokhanov cites, as an example, his collection of over $100,000 during a brief visit to the United States in the 1920s. See his *In the Cauldron of Russia*.

31. Funding for the 1926 Leningrad and 1927 Kiev Bibles (25,000 copies each) published for I. S. Prokhanov and Ya. I. Zhidkov in the new orthography (*Bibliya: Knigi svyashchennogo pisaniya vetkhogo i novogo zaveta. Kanonicheskie. V russkom perevode s parallel'nymi mestami*) came from the American Bible Society which contributed $15,000 toward the creation of a set of stereotype plates cast in Leningrad.

The type was set from the text of the 1907 Synod/BFBS co-operative edition. On this question, see Haven to Boughton, New York, 18 December 1925, BFBS Ed. Cor.: Russian, file 1.

32. Under repeated questioning about distribution of the Bibles, the All-Russian Union of Baptists did finally submit a list of churches and names to whom it had sent copies of BFBS scriptures. See 'Vedomost' na otpushchennye Biblii, Novye Zavety britanskogo izdaniya i evangelicheskie pesni bez not, s 1 Yanv. po 1 Apr. 1923 g.', BFBS Dep. Papers, The Wiseman Papers, file entitled 'A/Cs etc., Mr Paul Pavloff/Moscow Russian Baptists'. This list provides an interesting profile of where the Union of Baptists had churches within the Soviet Union.

33. Davidson to Rostron, Helsinki, 10 February 1922, BFBS Sec. Cor.: Russia, file 1a.

34. Ibid.

35. Davidson to Ritson, 9 March 1925, BFBS Dep. Papers, Wiseman Papers, file 2, Ritson Correspondence, 1920–6.

36. Pares to E. W. Smith, London, 5 February 1937, BFBS Ed. Cor., Russian, file 2.

37. Minutes of a Meeting of the Postwar Planning Special Subcommittee, 23 October 1941, in BFBS Ed. Cor., Russian, file 2.

38. The Bezsonov correspondence with the BFBS runs from 1946 to 1949, and includes an unpleasant exchange in *The Times* following BFBS abandonment of his project. See BFBS Ed. Cor., Russian, file 2. Bezsonov's escape from the USSR and conversion to Christianity can be followed in his two highly popular inter-war books: *Dvadtsat' shest' tyurem i pobeg s Solovkov* (Paris, 1928, and in English, London, 1929); and *Partiya sil'nykh* (Paris, 1942).

39. Bradnock to M. Beguin, 6 April 1950, BFBS Ed. Cor., Russian, file 3.

40. Copy of Anderson to North, 4 April 1950, BFBS Ed. Cor., Russian, file 3.

41. 'To the Members of the [BFBS] Translations and Library Subcommittee', by W. J. Bradnock, 2 October 1950, BFBS Ed. Cor., Russian, file 3.

42. Lowrie to Bradnock, Paris, 26 January 1951, and Bradnock

to Lowrie, London, 29 January 1951, BFBS Ed. Cor., Russian, file 3.

43. Copy of Patriarch Athenagoras to Bishop Cassian, Constantinople, 24 April 1951, BFBS Ed. Cor., Russian, file 3.

44. Correspondence regarding membership runs throughout the BFBS Ed. Cor., Russian, for the duration of the project. For an early and fairly complete list of members, see Lowrie to Bradnock, Paris, 22 February 1951, BFBS Ed. Cor., Russian, file 3.

45. The response of Russian evangelicals was carefully orchestrated, and the BFBS received form letter complaints from a large number of official organizations, such as the Slavic and Baltic Missionary Society and Slavic Gospel Association, Inc. The sheer number of responses makes the BFBS records significant as a sort of registry for Russian Protestantism in the West. On this and Wassilieff's inclusion on the committee, see BFBS Ed. Cor., Russian, file 3.

46. On pronominal capitalization, see BFBS Ed. Cor., Russian, file 4, 1952–3.

47. The regular minutes of the revision committee, interspersed throughout the BFBS Ed. Cor., Russian files, document Bishop Cassian's literalism. For the Gospel of John, see the microfilmed copy of Bishop Cassian's notes, BFBS Microfilm: 'Russian New Testament Notes of Bishop Cassian', 2 rolls, 1957–8.

48. The 1949 Nestle edition was used, *Novum Testamentum graece, cum apparatu critico curavit*, edited by Eberhard Nestle and Erwin Nestle, seventeenth edition (Stuttgart, 1949).

49. The opposition campaign waged in the pages of the *Zhurnal Moskovskoi Patryarkhii* (*ZMP*) included articles by I. Alekseev, 'K voprosu o novom perevode na russkii yazyk *Evangeliya ot Matfeya ZMP*, 2 (1954) 76–7; A. Osipov, 'K izdaniyu russkoi Biblii', *ZMP*, 8 (1955), 58–66, and 'Ob odnom novom zagranichnom izdanii russkoi Biblii', *ZMP*, 10 (1955), 48–53; and A. I. Ivanov, 'K voprosu o vosstanovlenii pervonachal'nogo grecheskogo teksta Novogo Zaveta', *ZMP*, 3 (1954), 38–50, 'Novyi perevod na russkii

yazyk *Evangeliya ot Matfeya'*, *ZMP*, 4 (1954), 45–55, and 5 (1954), 38–47, 'Novoe izdanie grecheskogo Novogo Zaveta [a review of the 1952 Nestle edition]', *ZMP*, 12 (1954), 69, and 'Novoe kriticheskoe izdanie grecheskogo teksta Novogo Zaveta', *ZMP*, 3 (1956), 49–58, 4, 49–58, and 5 (1956), 43–52. One of the more curious elements of the campaign was a short piece submitted by the leader of an Old Believer community, I. Vakon'ya, 'Bestsennoe bogatstvo russkikh perevodov Slova Bozhiya i tserkovnoi literatury', *ZMP*, 6 (1955), 65–7. One wonders about the Old Believer sensitivities of Vakon'ya when he writes, 'the love and sympathy of Old Believers must be completely on the side of the traditional Russian translation prepared for us by the Russian Orthodox Church'.

50. *Bibliya, ili Knigi Svyashchennogo Pisaniya Vetkhogo i Novogo Zaveta, v russkom perevode, s parallel'nymi mestami i ukazatelem tserkovnykh chtenii* (Moscow, 1956).

51. Bradnock to Wilkinson, London, 4 November 1955, BFBS Ed. Cor., Russian, file 9.

52. Anderson to Bradnock, Paris, 21 December 1960, BFBS Ed. Cor., Russian, file 9.

53. Elizabeth Pond, 'In Soviet Russia—A New Bible Translation', *Christian Science Monitor*, 22 June 1976, p. 14. Pond's article drew upon interviews with the Leningrad Academy Rector Bishop Kirill and others in Leningrad. Just at the time of Metropolitan Nikodim's death in 1978, a trial edition of the Gospel of John, translated in Leningrad by K. I. Logachev, was issued in the West as a part of the late Metropolitan's experiment (see *Evangelie po Ioannu v novom russkom perevode* (Brussels/United Bible Societies, 1978), especially the 'Predislovie', pp. iii–v).

54. Released from his Academy duties, Bishop Cassian took residence at the seaside resort community of Javea from whence his occasional correspondence to BFBS translations secretary W. J. Bradnock is dated. Upon completion of his draft translation from the Greek, Bishop Cassian became involved in his observer role at the Vatican Council. Subsequently, his failing health meant that committee revisions from about the Epistle to Galatians onward were done without the close oversight of the translator.

55. *Novyi Zavet Gospoda Nashego Iisusa Khrista* (London, 1970).
56. Sir Bernard Pares, 'Links with Russia: Points of Cultural Kinship', *Times Literary Supplement*, 6 September 1941, p. 429.

Foreign Collections and Soviet Archives: Russian Archaeographic Efforts in Great Britain and the Problem of Provenance

PATRICIA KENNEDY GRIMSTED

The wide-ranging importance of the survey under way of archival materials in the United Kingdom relating to Russia and the Soviet Union is highlighted by the papers of this conference. Such a project has a direct bearing on the study of relations between the Russian Empire/Soviet Union and Great Britain over the centuries, and gives many new perspectives into the nature and extent of interaction on the level of individuals, organizations and nation states. Similar surveys are needed in many countries, and the British example can further demonstrate the potential value of such an enterprise. The perspective I bring stems from my primary interest over the past twenty years in Soviet archives, and hence emphasizes the broader problems of provenance and inter-relationships that may emerge from the source base surveyed in Great Britain and the Russian/Soviet archival legacy remaining in the USSR.

A similar survey was completed in the United States under the auspices of the Kennan Institute during the 1970s. The publication of the resulting directory compiled by John Brown and Stephen Grant has opened up for Western researchers in Russian/Soviet area studies a wide range of hitherto untapped sources.[1] At the same time it has aroused tremendous interest among Soviet historians, archivists and curators, who are anxious for information about archival materials abroad relating to the history of the Russian Empire and the Soviet Union. For our Soviet colleagues, such surveys help to identify contingent materials that have migrated abroad through one channel or another, and which provide important links between sources available for a particular research topic or which shed new light on manuscripts now to be found in Soviet collections themselves. The relationship of documents in various locations must be carefully considered by the historian or literary scholar in many types of research. Only when we have complete surveys, archival inventories and collection catalogues does such a process become feasible.

The collaborative volume of documents published in 1980 by the United States National Archives and the Main Archival Administration of the Soviet Union serves as an example of the results that can be generated by such a survey when historians and archivists of both nations find ground for mutual co-operation in piecing together the documentation of their history.[2] From the Soviet side, a further practical result is the new survey of archival sources for American history, or more specifically Russian–American relations, now found in archives and manuscript collections in the USSR, compiled by one of the most prominent Soviet historians who participated in the initial documentary publication.[3]

Of course, in any survey of Russian archival materials abroad and in the determination of their relationship with archival materials now housed in the USSR, we should be aware at the outset that we are often going beyond the traditional sense of 'Russian' in an ethnic or linguistic meaning. Often in popular usage abroad, the term 'Russia' encompasses many non-Russian parts of the Russian Empire or the Soviet Union, yet in terms of the multiplicity of nationalities involved, we may be well faced with Polish, Estonian or Ukrainian sources as well as purely Russian ones. Consideration of the multi-ethnic dimensions of many collections will also lead us to consider other aspects of the problem of provenance, and to question to the extent to which we are dealing with Russian or Soviet sources rather than those relating to the Russian Empire or the Soviet Union.

When the historian considers the value for research purposes of Russian or Soviet sources uncovered abroad, traditional distinctions between different types of primary sources should be considered in conjunction with the provenance of materials involved. First, we must identify official documents such as treaties, charters or edicts, and then official diplomatic correspondence or journalistic reports filed in the field. All of these undoubtedly would become part of the official files or records produced by an institution or office in the normal course of its business. Secondly, we should identify primary accounts which might fall into the category of diaries, personal correspondence or journalist's notes. A third level of sources, somewhat further removed from the event, would encompass later recollections, memoirs, travel accounts or essays. Although the trained historian hardly needs to be reminded of such distinctions, their recognition in the context of the present discussion provides perspective for the evaluation and the practical use of the particular sources at hand.

The prospect of studying Russian history from British archival sources raises a number of practical and theoretical questions regarding the appropriateness and relative usefulness of such documentation. Do we have an adequate source base for the study of Russian history *per se*, or are we limited to the study of Britons in Russia or the study of Russians as foreigners in the context of a British experience? More broadly, are we limited to the treatment of Anglo-Russian relations, with emphasis on the British side, or can we penetrate and reconstruct the Russian side?

Given the source base uncovered by this survey in the United Kingdom, historians are going to find themselves for the most part faced with British documentation, as opposed to Russian primary documentation or official government records. The significance of the documentation available does not necessarily thereby diminish, provided the historian keeps an appropriate perspective regarding its use and authenticity. For indeed, in many cases, it may be the only data available, given current Soviet travel and archival restrictions. Although historians may thus often be limited to non-Russian perspectives, they may be able to follow the leads from documentation in their own country to uncover contingent materials now in the Soviet Union, or perhaps even in a third country, and thus ultimately obtain a wider source base for Russian history.

In reflecting on the nature of the more specific sources covered in the papers of this conference, one is struck by the extent to which this documentation has been created by British subjects not Russian. The travellers, journalists, businessmen, scientists, and even diplomats and military figures involved were Britons who spent some time, or in some cases became resident, in the Russian Empire or the Soviet Union. Thus unless the historian is interested purely in Britons in Russia, in the British side of Anglo-Russian relations, or more narrowly in the British view of Russia, the archival materials uncovered in the United Kingdom will most likely serve as only a small part of the sources needed for a particular topic. The historian satisfied only with documentation found outside the USSR will have an inadequate understanding of Russian history and culture without studying the related materials in Soviet archives and other manuscript repositories. Once the initial survey of sources outside the USSR has been completed, further more technical analysis is needed of the provenance of different materials, and their relationship to contingent bodies of documentation or existing record groups (*fonds*) within Soviet institutions.[4]

The most important major body of official government records in the United Kingdom are the various groups of diplomatic and consular records. These records, of course, constitute a primary source for the reconstruction of Anglo-Russian diplomatic relations through the centuries. The use of these records for the internal history of Russia is more limited. Even for foreign relations, without the corresponding Russian Foreign Ministry records in Moscow, the historian will have only one side of the story. In the case of Russian diplomatic and consular records, all extant materials going back to the beginning of the eighteenth century have now been centralized under the Archival Administration of the Soviet Foreign Ministry. Regrettably, however, no guides have been published either by the pre-revolutionary Archive of Russian Foreign Policy (Arkhiv vneshnei politiki Rossii), or the post-revolutionary equivalent (Arkhiv vneshnei politiki SSSR).[5]

Only two major campaigns involving British and Russian forces are well documented from the British side. There are significant groups of British military records in the United Kingdom relating to the Crimean War and the Allied military intervention during the Civil War. In terms of the corresponding Russian materials, pre-revolutionary records relating to military affairs in the Russian Empire have been centralized in the Central State Military History Archive (Tsentral'nyi gosudarstvennyi voenno-istoricheskii arkhiv SSR), but the only available guide, published in 1941, is now severely out of date.[6] Post-revolutionary military records for the period to the 1930s have been centralized in the Central State Archive of the Soviet Army (Tsentral'nyi gosudarstvennyi arkhiv Sovetskoi armii).[7] Not even a preliminary description has been published of the main archive for the Second World War military records under the Ministry of Defence in Podol'sk outside Moscow.

Business records constitute another category of records and could prove of great importance for the historian dealing with Anglo-Russian relations. Of most interest to the historian of Russian history are the records of British firms operating businesses in Russia. Significant portions of those records might remain in the Soviet Union so that the scholar might need the contingent materials in Soviet archives to put his subject in perspective. Business records are widely scattered in Soviet repositories, although the researcher is aided by the extent to which extant archival records have all been taken over by the state since the Revolution. Records of banks, business firms, factories, and other commercial institutions or organizations all tend to be preserved in local state archives, in the present state archival centre which serves their former place of operation. Except in the case of particularly large and noteworthy firms, they are most likely to be found in local state *oblast'* level archives, now located in the present *oblast'* centre. Likewise, local customs house records are likely to be in the local archives of the ports involved, or in the neighbouring *oblast'* centre if the port is not now an *oblast'* or union-republic capital. Records from the Baltic ports, which were particularly important for trade with Great Britain, are now found in city archives or in the central state historical archives of the present-day Soviet Baltic republics.[8]

In piecing together the story of Anglo-Russian business and commercial relations, the historian has to keep in mind the extent of state control over business contacts with foreign firms in both the Russian Empire and the Soviet Union. Hence the historian may well have to go beyond the extant, and often fragmentary, business records that might be preserved, to the records of pertinent ministries, state financial institutions, or even cabinet-level officials, that might have been involved in the authorization or facilitation of the enterprise. In the case of shipping and other commercial records, the historian also will be led in many cases to third-party records, as in the case of triangular trade routes or shipping under the flag of other nations. Of course, commercial or customs files may well be connected with consular records. Further complexities arise in some periods when resident businessmen might have been serving in consular roles.

Relevant archival links for left-wing political contacts are most likely to be held in the archives of the Communist Party of the Soviet Union. Relevant materials among the records of the British Communist Party and left-wing organizations are likely to find their counterparts in Party archive records in Moscow, and particularly in the records of the Communist International in various periods. However, initial reports of the British archival survey suggest that extant Communist Party documentation on the British side is sparse. Significant holdings relating to the Soviet Union were reported by the Labour Party Archive, but other left-wing parties and trade unions in Great Britain report fewer relevant sources.

Important groups of missionary records have come to light, but in terms of religion in the Russian Empire, the historian is dealing with a minor part of Russian religious life. No major groups of institutional records available in Great Britain pertain directly to the Russian Orthodox Church, the Greek Catholic (Uniate) Church or Jewish communities in the Russian Empire. Hence it is hard for the historian to deal with Russian church history, except in terms of interaction with foreign evangelical, and predominantly Protestant, missionary activities. Anglo-Soviet relations in the religious realm are also difficult to trace from the Soviet side because, in recent decades, detailed inventorying and descriptive work for church records has not had a high priority within Soviet state archival institutions, although all church archives have been taken over by the state since the Revolution.

The problems of tracing contacts in the scientific and cultural realm are likely to entail an archival search into other directions. The autonomy of the Russian, and later Soviet, Academy of Sciences, along with the academies of sciences of the various union republics, has meant that their archives, too, have always remained independent from direct state archival administration control. In many cases these institutions have remained the most responsive to foreign enquiries, and the high quality of the inventory work accomplished for their records facilitates the task of the researcher.[9] Archives of various universities, museums and other scientific or cultural organizations may also yield relevant documentation in the search for contingent records of Anglo-Soviet contacts in these realms. These are widely scattered predominantly in local repositories.

Personal papers deposited in British repositories of individuals who had extensive contact or residence in the Russian Empire/Soviet Union are a rich body of documentation for Russian history. In dealing with personal papers, the distinction must always be made between the individual's own papers and materials that he has collected. Britons long resident in Russia, or even more casual visitors, were often collectors, and in some cases their collections of historical documentation may prove more important than their own papers.

Émigré papers in the United Kingdom require a clear line of demarcation between materials that were created in the Russian Empire/USSR and hence of Russian/Soviet provenance and those which were created in emigration. Usually papers transported abroad resulting from the individual's activities before departure from Russia are likely to be much less voluminous than those actually created abroad. Yet, of course, papers of Russians abroad may well contain important correspondence from their friends and colleagues in their home country. Although the line of demarcation in terms of provenance may be blurred in some cases, the distinction should not be overlooked by the researcher who may be using these papers as sources. A somewhat different perspective is needed in the case of papers in British collections of prominent individuals of foreign origin who spent long periods in Russian service. A prime example is the impressive collection of Lieven papers in the Manuscript Department of the British Library, which contain a wide range of diplomatic and personal correspondence along with copies of official diplomatic dispatches and other documentation from the early nineteenth century.[10]

Personal papers themselves need to be analysed in connection with correspondence remaining among the personal papers located in Soviet collections. The task of their location in the USSR has been facilitated by the nationalization of personal papers of political and cultural leaders and the preparation of an extensive all-union directory.[11] It is to be hoped that future supplementary volumes to that directory will provide broader coverage and mention many of the individuals and families known to have been omitted from the volumes already published.

Historians trying to trace contiguous archival materials of non-Russian provenance may encounter a number of special problems. However, a better understanding of the current Soviet state archival organization with regard to non-Russian republics will assist the researcher in knowing where to search.[12] While the emphasis of the survey taking place at the School of Slavonic and East European Studies has been on Russian materials, coverage does extend to many non-Russian materials from areas within the Russian Empire and now the Soviet Union.

In the case of émigré community archives and émigré collections from non-Russian ethnic groups now settled in the United Kingdom, the distinction has to be made between materials created in the present territory of the USSR and those created in emigration. The whole subject of non-Russian materials, particularly those involving such extensive national groups in emigration, such as Ukrainians, Belorussians and the Baltic peoples, should eventually be given separate consideration, although invariably there is considerable overlap with any survey of Russian materials in the United Kingdom. Understandable political sensitivity surrounds remaining records from the independent Baltic states during the inter-war period. By established international law and diplomatic practice, such groups of records technically belong to the successor state. However, despite the subsequent annexation of these areas by the Soviet Union, various political or personal reasons preclude their revindication.

Co-ordination between archival materials abroad and those in the Soviet Union is likely to be most difficult in the case of fragmentary documentary collections, where scattered documents or archival materials have been dislodged from their integral archival groups. Autographs of famous literary and/or historical figures have always been popular for collectors, and some have come into groups of personal papers through personal contacts and correspondence with the individuals involved. Early historical documents, such as parchment charters and miscellaneous documentation from various sources, are often found in both personal papers and miscellaneous collections. In some cases the trail of their migration is a lengthy one, and their cash value in the antiquarian market has often led to their further migration and detachment from the original body of archival records to which they belonged. Careful cataloguing and descriptive work can help, but many of these materials that are now scattered widely in British collections are going to be the most difficult to identify with an adequate degree of precision in terms of their actual provenance.

Medieval Slavonic manuscript books present a special problem within the realm of Russian archival materials and are appropriately being dealt with in a separate cataloguing effort, as described by R. Cleminson. Many of the early Slavonic manuscript books now available in the United Kingdom came as a result of the collecting efforts of individuals who spent some time in Russia, although in other cases they may have been brought out by third parties and acquired abroad. Various religious texts and manuscript codices need to be identified not only in terms of their original provenance and earlier migration but also in terms of other copies or redactions within a particular manuscript tradition. International cataloguing standards and co-ordination with various ongoing projects of Slavonic manuscript description will facilitate the task.

The general problem of trying to co-ordinate Russian archival remains in the United Kingdom with the parent record groups or archives in the Soviet Union itself raises the further problem of access to Soviet archives for British scholars. The difficulty for foreigners of travelling to the Soviet Union and of gaining access not only to archives and manuscript repositories there, but also to adequate finding aids, are the greatest obstacles to the historian's task of documenting Anglo-Russian contacts and Russian history. If the experience of various American and West European projects can be seen as an example, Soviet authorities may be expected to be more willing to assist with topics and with archival investigations when it is a matter of British scholars seeking British and British-related documentation in Soviet

institutions. The experience of foreign scholars attempting research in the Soviet Union suggests that more obstacles will arise
for research and topics in internal Russian history than with the
foreign nationals' concern to match up or correlate materials
already uncovered and identified abroad.

Thus we come back full circle to the value of the survey being
undertaken now of archival materials relating to Russia and the
Soviet Union in the United Kingdom. Although the materials uncovered will be predominantly British documentation, which can
shed most light on the British aspects of Anglo-Russian relations,
Russian historians, or historians of Russia and the Soviet Union,
will profit from the knowledge of sources abroad, which in turn may
help to compensate for the difficulties of access to materials in
Soviet collections. The process of trying to find contingent materials
within Soviet archival institutions may well encourage historical
studies abroad to move in new directions through a wider knowledge of sources for Russian history. Such results serve to reinforce
the hope that this survey of archival materials in the United
Kingdom will provide an example for similar work in other
countries, all of which will expand our knowledge of sources for
the study of Russian history, and for Slavic studies more generally.

Notes

1.   Steven A. Grant and John H. Brown, *The Russian Empire
     and Soviet Union: A Guide to Manuscripts and Archival
     Materials in the United States* (Boston, 1981). My participa-
     tion in launching the project and serving as a consultant in
     its initial stages grew out of my experience in Soviet ar-
     chives and my concern about the description and preserv-
     ation of related materials abroad.
2.   *The United States and Russia: The Beginning of Relations,
     1765–1815*, edited by Nina N. Bashkina, Nikolai N.
     Bolkhovitinov, John H. Brown *et al.* (Washington, DC,
     1980). *Rossiya i SShA: Stanovlenie otnoshenii, 1765–1815*
     (Moscow, 1980). Serving as a consultant to this project for
     the American side gave me further perspective on the
     types of sources available from archives and manuscript
     collections in both countries, and the types of problems
     involved in piecing together their inter-relationship.

3.   N. N. Bolkhovitinov, *Rossiya i SShA: Arkhivnye dokumenty i istoricheskie issledovaniya. Analiticheskii obzor* (Moscow, 1984). An English version, translated by J. Dane Hartgrove, is in preparation for a forthcoming issue of *Soviet Studies in History*.

4.   For a directory and bibliography of finding aids, see my *Archives and Manuscript Repositories in the USSR: Moscow and Leningrad* (Princeton, NJ, 1972) and *Supplement 1. Bibliographical Addenda* (Zug, 1976). More recent, selected literature published in 1980–1 is mentioned in my article, 'Recent Publications on Archives and Manuscript Collections in the Soviet Union: A Selective Survey', *Slavic Review*, 41 (fall 1982), 511–33. Institutions outside Moscow and Leningrad are covered in my *Archives and Manuscript Repositories in the USSR: Estonia, Latvia, Lithuania, and Belorussia* (Princeton, NJ, 1981) and *Archives and Manuscript Repositories in the USSR: Ukraine and Moldavia*, Part 1: *General Bibliography and Institutional Directory* (Princeton, NJ, forthcoming). The most important single Soviet publication for the archival researcher is *Spravochnik nauchnogo rabotnika: Arkhivy, dokumenty, issledovatel'*, edited by Ya. M. Grossman and V. N. Kutik, 2nd edition (Lviv, 1983).

5.   See the relevant information in my *Archives: Moscow and Leningrad*, pp. 248–55.

6.   A new directory, *Tsentral'nyi gosudarstvennyi voenno-istoricheskii arkhiv SSSR. Putevoditel'*, 3 vols (Moscow, 1979), was published in a three-volume *rotaprint* edition in 1979, but unfortunately was issued for internal use only, and hence not even available to the public in Soviet libraries. For additional information, see my *Archives: Moscow and Leningrad*, pp. 183–9, and Grossman and Kutik, *Spravochnik*, pp. 29–30.

7.   See *Archives: Moscow and Leningrad*, pp. 135–7, and *Spravochnik*, pp. 30–2.

8.   See details in my directory of Baltic archives cited above.

9.   See the appropriate sections in my directories cited above for introductory surveys and bibliography of finding aids regarding the archives of the Academies of Sciences. See also the helpful new directory volume, *Kratkii spravochnik*

po nauchno-otraslevym i memorial'nym arkhivam AN SSSR, edited by B. V. Levshin (Moscow, 1979), as well as more recent reference literature published by the archives of the Soviet Academy of Sciences.

10.   Papers of Christopher A. Lieven (1777–1839), along with those of his wife, Dariya (*née* Benckendorff; 1784–1857), are in the British Library, Add. MSS 47236–435.

11.   *Lichnye arkhivnye fondy v gosudarstvennykh khranilishchakh SSSR. Ukazatel'* (Moscow, 1962–3, 1980), a three-volume directory listing personal papers in archives and manuscript collections throughout the Soviet Union. However, researchers should be aware that this directory omits papers of politically sensitive individuals, Communist Party archives, and the papers of pre-Soviet non-Russian individuals in areas subsequently annexed to the Soviet Union, such as the Baltic countries and Western Ukraine. Although the directory does not list correspondents within the *fondy* of personal papers, such data may often be found in the guides to particular archives or other manuscript repositories where the papers are now held.

12.   See my articles 'Regional Archival Developments in the USSR: Soviet Standards and National Documentary Legacies', *American Archivist*, 36 (January 1973), 43–66, and 'Regional State Archives in the USSR: Some Notes and a Bibliography of Published Guides', *Slavic Review*, 28 (March 1969), 94–6. These are now somewhat dated. Coverage of the Soviet Baltic, Belorussian and Ukrainian republics has been extended in my directories listed in note 4 above.